DICTIONARY
THEME–BASED

ENGLISH-
UKRAINIAN

The most useful words
To expand your lexicon and sharpen
your language skills

3000 words

Theme-based dictionary British English-Ukrainian - 3000 words
By Andrey Taranov

T&P Books vocabularies are intended for helping you learn, memorize and review foreign words. The dictionary is divided into themes, covering all major spheres of everyday activities, business, science, culture, etc.

The process of learning words using T&P Books' theme-based dictionaries gives you the following advantages:

- Correctly grouped source information predetermines success at subsequent stages of word memorization
- Availability of words derived from the same root allowing memorization of word units (rather than separate words)
- Small units of words facilitate the process of establishing associative links needed for consolidation of vocabulary
- Level of language knowledge can be estimated by the number of learned words

T&P Books Publishing
www.tpbooks.com

This book is also available in E-book formats.
Please visit www.tpbooks.com or the major online bookstores.

UKRAINIAN THEME-BASED DICTIONARY
British English collection

T&P Books vocabularies are intended to help you learn, memorize, and review foreign words. The vocabulary contains over 3000 commonly used words arranged thematically.

- Vocabulary contains the most commonly used words
- Recommended as an addition to any language course
- Meets the needs of beginners and advanced learners of foreign languages
- Convenient for daily use, revision sessions, and self-testing activities
- Allows you to assess your vocabulary

Special features of the vocabulary

- Words are organized according to their meaning, not alphabetically
- Words are presented in three columns to facilitate the reviewing and self-testing processes
- Words in groups are divided into small blocks to facilitate the learning process
- The vocabulary offers a convenient and simple transcription of each foreign word

The vocabulary has 101 topics including:

Basic Concepts, Numbers, Colors, Months, Seasons, Units of Measurement, Clothing & Accessories, Food & Nutrition, Restaurant, Family Members, Relatives, Character, Feelings, Emotions, Diseases, City, Town, Sightseeing, Shopping, Money, House, Home, Office, Working in the Office, Import & Export, Marketing, Job Search, Sports, Education, Computer, Internet, Tools, Nature, Countries, Nationalities and more ...

TABLE OF CONTENTS

FLORA

COUNTRIES OF THE WORLD

PRONUNCIATION GUIDE

Letter	Ukrainian example	T&P phonetic alphabet	English example

Vowels

Letter	Ukrainian example	T&P phonetic alphabet	English example
А а	акт	[a]	shorter than in 'ask'
Е е	берет	[e], [ɛ]	absent, pet
Є є	модельєр	[ɛ]	man, bad
И и	ритм	[k]	clock, kiss
І і	компанія	[i]	shorter than in 'feet'
Ї ї	поїзд	[ji]	playing, spying
О о	око	[ɔ]	bottle, doctor
У у	буря	[u]	book
Ю ю	костюм	[ʲu]	cued, cute
Я я	маяк	[ja], [ʲa]	royal

Consonants

Letter	Ukrainian example	T&P phonetic alphabet	English example
Б б	бездна	[b]	baby, book
В в	вікно	[w]	vase, winter
Г г	готель	[h]	between [g] and [h]
Ґ ґ	ґудзик	[g]	game, gold
Д д	дефіс	[d]	day, doctor
Ж ж	жанр	[ʒ]	forge, pleasure
З з	зброя	[z]	zebra, please
Й й	йти	[j]	yes, New York
К к	крок	[k]	clock, kiss
Л л	лев	[l]	lace, people
М м	мати	[m]	magic, milk
Н н	назва	[n]	name, normal
П п	приз	[p]	pencil, private
Р р	радість	[r]	rice, radio
С с	сон	[s]	city, boss
Т т	тир	[t]	tourist, trip
Ф ф	фарба	[f]	face, food
Х х	холод	[h]	home, have
Ц ц	церква	[ts]	cats, tsetse fly
Ч ч	час	[tʃ]	church, French
Ш ш	шуба	[ʃ]	machine, shark
Щ щ	щука	[ɕ]	sheep, shop
ь	камінь	[ʲ]	soft sign - no sound
ъ	ім'я	[ʲ]	hard sign, no sound

ABBREVIATIONS
used in the dictionary

English abbreviations

ab.	-	about
adj	-	adjective
adv	-	adverb
anim.	-	animate
as adj	-	attributive noun used as adjective
e.g.	-	for example
etc.	-	et cetera
fam.	-	familiar
fem.	-	feminine
form.	-	formal
inanim.	-	inanimate
masc.	-	masculine
math	-	mathematics
mil.	-	military
n	-	noun
pl	-	plural
pron.	-	pronoun
sb	-	somebody
sing.	-	singular
sth	-	something
v aux	-	auxiliary verb
vi	-	intransitive verb
vi, vt	-	intransitive, transitive verb
vt	-	transitive verb

Ukrainian abbreviations

ж	-	feminine noun
мн	-	plural
с	-	neuter
ч	-	masculine noun

BASIC CONCEPTS

1. Pronouns

I, me	я	[ja]
you	ти	[ti]
he	він	[win]
she	вона	[wo'na]
we	ми	[mi]
you (to a group)	ви	[wi̇]
they	вони	[wo'ni̇]

2. Greetings. Salutations

Hello! (fam.)	Здрастуй!	['zdrastuj]
Hello! (form.)	Здрастуйте!	['zdrastujtɛ]
Good morning!	Доброго ранку!	['dɔbroɦo 'ranku]
Good afternoon!	Добрий день!	['dɔbrij dɛnʲ]
Good evening!	Добрий вечір!	['dɔbrij 'wɛʧir]
to say hello	вітатися	[wi'tatisʲa]
Hi! (hello)	Привіт!	[pri'wit]
greeting (n)	вітання (c)	[wi'tanʲa]
to greet (vt)	вітати	[wi'tati]
How are you?	Як справи?	[jak 'sprawi̇]
What's new?	Що нового?	[ɕo no'woɦo]
Bye-Bye! Goodbye!	До побачення!	[do po'baʧɛnʲa]
See you soon!	До швидкої зустрічі!	[do ʃwid'kojɨ 'zustriʧi]
Farewell! (to a friend)	Прощавай!	[proɕa'waj]
Farewell! (form.)	Прощавайте!	[proɕa'wajtɛ]
to say goodbye	прощатися	[pro'ɕatisʲa]
Cheers!	Бувай!	[bu'waj]
Thank you! Cheers!	Дякую!	['dʲakuʲu]
Thank you very much!	Щиро дякую!	['ɕiro 'dʲakuʲu]
My pleasure!	Будь ласка.	[budʲ 'laska]
Don't mention it!	Не варто подяки	[nɛ 'warto po'dʲaki]
It was nothing	Нема за що.	[nɛ'ma za ɕo]
Excuse me! (fam.)	Вибач!	['wibaʧ]
Excuse me! (form.)	Вибачте!	['wibaʧtɛ]
to excuse (forgive)	вибачати	[wiba'ʧati]
to apologize (vi)	вибачатися	[wiba'ʧatisʲa]
My apologies	Моє вибачення.	[mo'ɛ 'wibaʧɛnʲa]

I'm sorry!	Вибачте!	['wɪbatʃtɛ]
to forgive (vt)	пробачати	[proba'tʃati]
please (adv)	будь ласка	[budʲ 'laska]

Don't forget!	Не забудьте!	[nɛ za'budʲtɛ]
Certainly!	Звичайно!	[zwi'tʃajno]
Of course not!	Звичайно ні!	[zwi'tʃajno ni]
Okay! (I agree)	Згоден!	['zɦɔdɛn]
That's enough!	Досить!	['dɔsitʲ]

3. Questions

Who?	Хто?	[hto]
What?	Що?	[ɕo]
Where? (at, in)	Де?	[dɛ]
Where (to)?	Куди?	[ku'dɪ]
From where?	Звідки?	['zwidkɪ]
When?	Коли?	[ko'lɪ]
Why? (What for?)	Навіщо?	[na'wiɕo]
Why? (~ are you crying?)	Чому?	[tʃo'mu]

What for?	Для чого?	[dlʲa 'tʃoɦo]
How? (in what way)	Як?	[jak]
What? (What kind of ...?)	Який?	[ja'kij]
Which?	Котрий?	[kot'rij]

To whom?	Кому?	[ko'mu]
About whom?	Про кого?	[pro 'koɦo]
About what?	Про що?	[pro ɕo]
With whom?	З ким?	[z kim]

| How many? How much? | Скільки? | ['skilʲkɪ] |
| Whose? | Чий? | [tʃij] |

4. Prepositions

with (accompanied by)	з	[z]
without	без	[bɛz]
to (indicating direction)	в	[w]
about (talking ~ ...)	про	[pro]
before (in time)	перед	['pɛrɛd]
in front of ...	перед	['pɛrɛd]

under (beneath, below)	під	[pid]
above (over)	над	[nad]
on (atop)	над	[nad]

| from (off, out of) | з | [z] |
| of (made from) | з | [z] |

| in (e.g. ~ ten minutes) | за | [za] |
| over (across the top of) | через | ['tʃɛrɛz] |

5. Function words. Adverbs. Part 1

Where? (at, in)	Де?	[dɛ]
here (adv)	тут	[tut]
there (adv)	там	[tam]
somewhere (to be)	десь	[dɛsʲ]
nowhere (not in any place)	ніде	[ni'dɛ]
by (near, beside)	біля	['bilʲa]
by the window	біля вікна	['bilʲa wik'na]
Where (to)?	Куди?	[ku'dɨ]
here (e.g. come ~!)	сюди	[sʲu'dɨ]
there (e.g. to go ~)	туди	[tu'dɨ]
from here (adv)	звідси	['zwidsɨ]
from there (adv)	звідти	['zwidtɨ]
close (adv)	близько	['blizʲko]
far (adv)	далеко	[da'lɛko]
near (e.g. ~ Paris)	біля	['bilʲa]
nearby (adv)	поряд	['pɔrʲad]
not far (adv)	недалеко	[nɛda'lɛko]
left (adj)	лівий	['liwɨj]
on the left	зліва	['zliwa]
to the left	ліворуч	[li'wɔrutʃ]
right (adj)	правий	['prawɨj]
on the right	справа	['sprawa]
to the right	праворуч	[pra'wɔrutʃ]
in front (adv)	спереду	['spɛrɛdu]
front (as adj)	передній	[pɛ'rɛdnij]
ahead (the kids ran ~)	уперед	[upɛ'rɛd]
behind (adv)	позаду	[po'zadu]
from behind	ззаду	['zzadu]
back (towards the rear)	назад	[na'zad]
middle	середина (ж)	[sɛ'rɛdɨna]
in the middle	посередині	[posɛ'rɛdɨni]
at the side	збоку	['zbɔku]
everywhere (adv)	скрізь	[skrizʲ]
around (in all directions)	навколо	[naw'kɔlo]
from inside	зсередини	[zsɛ'rɛdɨni]
somewhere (to go)	кудись	[ku'dɨsʲ]
straight (directly)	напрямки	[naprʲam'kɨ]
back (e.g. come ~)	назад	[na'zad]
from anywhere	звідки-небудь	['zwidkɨ 'nɛbudʲ]
from somewhere	звідкись	['zwidkɨsʲ]

firstly (adv)	по-перше	[po 'pɛrʃɛ]
secondly (adv)	по-друге	[po 'druɦɛ]
thirdly (adv)	по-третє	[po t'rɛtɛ]
suddenly (adv)	раптом	['raptom]
at first (in the beginning)	спочатку	[spo'ʧatku]
for the first time	уперше	[u'pɛrʃɛ]
long before ...	задовго до ...	[za'dɔwɦo do]
anew (over again)	заново	['zanowo]
for good (adv)	назовсім	[na'zɔwsim]
never (adv)	ніколи	[ni'kɔli]
again (adv)	знову	['znɔwu]
now (at present)	тепер	[tɛ'pɛr]
often (adv)	часто	['ʧasto]
then (adv)	тоді	[to'di]
urgently (quickly)	терміново	[tɛrmi'nɔwo]
usually (adv)	звичайно	[zwɨ'ʧajno]
by the way, ...	до речі	[do 'rɛʧi]
possibly	можливо	[moʒ'lɨwo]
probably (adv)	мабуть	[ma'butʲ]
maybe (adv)	може бути	['mɔʒɛ 'butɨ]
besides ...	крім того, ...	[krim 'tɔɦo]
that's why ...	тому	[to'mu]
in spite of ...	незважаючи на ...	[nɛzwa'ʒaʲutʃɨ na]
thanks to ...	завдяки ...	[zawdʲa'kɨ]
what (pron.)	що	[ɕo]
that (conj.)	що	[ɕo]
something	щось	[ɕosʲ]
anything (something)	що-небудь	[ɕo 'nɛbudʲ]
nothing	нічого	[ni'ʧɔɦo]
who (pron.)	хто	[hto]
someone	хтось	[htosʲ]
somebody	хто-небудь	[hto 'nɛbudʲ]
nobody	ніхто	[nih'tɔ]
nowhere (a voyage to ~)	нікуди	['nikudɨ]
nobody's	нічий	[ni'ʧɨj]
somebody's	чий-небудь	[ʧɨj 'nɛbudʲ]
so (I'm ~ glad)	так	[tak]
also (as well)	також	[ta'kɔʒ]
too (as well)	також	[ta'kɔʒ]

6. Function words. Adverbs. Part 2

Why?	Чому?	[ʧo'mu]
for some reason	чомусь	[ʧo'musʲ]
because ...	тому, що ...	[to'mu, ɕo ...]
for some purpose	навіщось	[na'wiɕosʲ]
and	і	[i]

or	або	[a'bɔ]
but	але	[a'lɛ]
for (e.g. ~ me)	для	[dlʲa]
too (excessively)	занадто	[za'nadto]
only (exclusively)	тільки	['tilʲki]
exactly (adv)	точно	['tɔʧno]
about (more or less)	приблизно	[prib'lizno]
approximately (adv)	приблизно	[prib'lizno]
approximate (adj)	приблизний	[prib'liznij]
almost (adv)	майже	['majʒɛ]
the rest	решта (ж)	['rɛʃta]
each (adj)	кожен	['kɔʒɛn]
any (no matter which)	будь-який	[budʲ ja'kij]
many, much (a lot of)	багато	[ba'hato]
many people	багато хто	[ba'hato hto]
all (everyone)	всі	[wsi]
in return for ...	в обмін на ...	[w 'ɔbmin na]
in exchange (adv)	натомість	[na'tɔmistʲ]
by hand (made)	вручну	[wruʧ'nu]
hardly (negative opinion)	навряд чи	[naw'rʲad ʧi]
probably (adv)	мабуть	[ma'butʲ]
on purpose (intentionally)	навмисно	[naw'misno]
by accident (adv)	випадково	[wipad'kɔwo]
very (adv)	дуже	['duʒɛ]
for example (adv)	наприклад	[na'priklad]
between	між	[miʒ]
among	серед	['sɛrɛd]
so much (such a lot)	стільки	['stilʲki]
especially (adv)	особливо	[osob'liwo]

NUMBERS. MISCELLANEOUS

7. Cardinal numbers. Part 1

0 zero	нуль	[nulʲ]
1 one	один	[oˈdɨn]
2 two	два	[dwa]
3 three	три	[trɨ]
4 four	чотири	[ʧoˈtɨrɨ]

5 five	п'ять	[pʲˈatʲ]
6 six	шість	[ʃistʲ]
7 seven	сім	[sim]
8 eight	вісім	[ˈwisim]
9 nine	дев'ять	[ˈdɛwʲatʲ]

10 ten	десять	[ˈdɛsʲatʲ]
11 eleven	одинадцять	[odɨˈnadʦʲatʲ]
12 twelve	дванадцять	[dwaˈnadʦʲatʲ]
13 thirteen	тринадцять	[trɨˈnadʦʲatʲ]
14 fourteen	чотирнадцять	[ʧotɨrˈnadʦʲatʲ]

15 fifteen	п'ятнадцять	[pʲatˈnadʦʲatʲ]
16 sixteen	шістнадцять	[ʃistˈnadʦʲatʲ]
17 seventeen	сімнадцять	[simˈnadʦʲatʲ]
18 eighteen	вісімнадцять	[wisimˈnadʦʲatʲ]
19 nineteen	дев'ятнадцять	[dɛwʲatˈnadʦʲatʲ]

20 twenty	двадцять	[ˈdwadʦʲatʲ]
21 twenty-one	двадцять один	[ˈdwadʦʲatʲ oˈdɨn]
22 twenty-two	двадцять два	[ˈdwadʦʲatʲ dwa]
23 twenty-three	двадцять три	[ˈdwadʦʲatʲ trɨ]

30 thirty	тридцять	[ˈtrɨdʦʲatʲ]
31 thirty-one	тридцять один	[ˈtrɨdʦʲatʲ oˈdɨn]
32 thirty-two	тридцять два	[ˈtrɨdʦʲatʲ dwa]
33 thirty-three	тридцять три	[ˈtrɨdʦʲatʲ trɨ]

40 forty	сорок	[ˈsɔrok]
41 forty-one	сорок один	[ˈsɔrok oˈdɨn]
42 forty-two	сорок два	[ˈsɔrok dwa]
43 forty-three	сорок три	[ˈsɔrok trɨ]

50 fifty	п'ятдесят	[pʲatdɛˈsʲat]
51 fifty-one	п'ятдесят один	[pʲatdɛˈsʲat oˈdɨn]
52 fifty-two	п'ятдесят два	[pʲatdɛˈsʲat dwa]
53 fifty-three	п'ятдесят три	[pʲatdɛˈsʲat trɨ]

| 60 sixty | шістдесят | [ʃizdɛˈsʲat] |
| 61 sixty-one | шістдесят один | [ʃizdɛˈsʲat oˈdɨn] |

| 62 sixty-two | шістдесят два | [ʃizdɛ'sʲat dwa] |
| 63 sixty-three | шістдесят три | [ʃizdɛ'sʲat tri] |

70 seventy	сімдесят	[simdɛ'sʲat]
71 seventy-one	сімдесят один	[simdɛ'sʲat odin]
72 seventy-two	сімдесят два	[simdɛ'sʲat dwa]
73 seventy-three	сімдесят три	[simdɛ'sʲat tri]

80 eighty	вісімдесят	[wisimdɛ'sʲat]
81 eighty-one	вісімдесят один	[wisimdɛ'sʲat o'din]
82 eighty-two	вісімдесят два	[wisimdɛ'sʲat dwa]
83 eighty-three	вісімдесят три	[wisimdɛ'sʲat tri]

90 ninety	дев'яносто	[dɛwʲa'nɔsto]
91 ninety-one	дев'яносто один	[dɛwʲa'nɔsto o'din]
92 ninety-two	дев'яносто два	[dɛwʲa'nɔsto dwa]
93 ninety-three	дев'яносто три	[dɛwʲa'nɔsto tri]

8. Cardinal numbers. Part 2

100 one hundred	сто	[sto]
200 two hundred	двісті	['dwisti]
300 three hundred	триста	['trista]
400 four hundred	чотириста	[tʃo'tirista]
500 five hundred	п'ятсот	[pʲa'tsɔt]

600 six hundred	шістсот	[ʃist'sɔt]
700 seven hundred	сімсот	[sim'sɔt]
800 eight hundred	вісімсот	[wisim'sɔt]
900 nine hundred	дев'ятсот	[dɛwʲa'tsɔt]

1000 one thousand	тисяча	['tisʲatʃa]
2000 two thousand	дві тисячі	[dwi 'tisʲatʃi]
3000 three thousand	три тисячі	[tri 'tisʲatʃi]
10000 ten thousand	десять тисяч	['dɛsʲatʲ 'tisʲatʃ]
one hundred thousand	сто тисяч	[sto 'tisʲatʃ]
million	мільйон (ч)	[milʲ'jɔn]
billion	мільярд (ч)	[mi'ljard]

9. Ordinal numbers

first (adj)	перший	['pɛrʃij]
second (adj)	другий	['druɦij]
third (adj)	третій	['trɛtij]
fourth (adj)	четвертий	[tʃɛt'wɛrtij]
fifth (adj)	п'ятий	['pʲatij]

sixth (adj)	шостий	['ʃɔstij]
seventh (adj)	сьомий	['sʲɔmij]
eighth (adj)	восьмий	['wɔsʲmij]
ninth (adj)	дев'ятий	[dɛ'wʲatij]
tenth (adj)	десятий	[dɛ'sʲatij]

COLORS. UNITS OF MEASUREMENT

10. Colours

colour	колір (ч)	['kɔlir]
shade (tint)	відтінок (ч)	[wid'tinok]
hue	тон (ч)	[ton]
rainbow	веселка (ж)	[wɛ'sɛlka]
white (adj)	білий	['bilij]
black (adj)	чорний	['ʧɔrnij]
grey (adj)	сірий	['sirij]
green (adj)	зелений	[zɛ'lɛnij]
yellow (adj)	жовтий	['ʒɔwtij]
red (adj)	червоний	[ʧɛr'wɔnij]
blue (adj)	синій	['sinij]
light blue (adj)	блакитний	[bla'kitnij]
pink (adj)	рожевий	[ro'ʒɛwij]
orange (adj)	помаранчевий	[poma'ranʧɛwij]
violet (adj)	фіолетовий	[fio'lɛtowij]
brown (adj)	коричневий	[ko'riʧnɛwij]
golden (adj)	золотий	[zolo'tij]
silvery (adj)	сріблястий	[srib'lʲastij]
beige (adj)	бежевий	['bɛʒɛwij]
cream (adj)	кремовий	['krɛmowij]
turquoise (adj)	бірюзовий	[birʲu'zɔwij]
cherry red (adj)	вишневий	[wiʃ'nɛwij]
lilac (adj)	бузковий	[buz'kɔwij]
crimson (adj)	малиновий	[ma'linowij]
light (adj)	світлий	['switlij]
dark (adj)	темний	['tɛmnij]
bright, vivid (adj)	яскравий	[jas'krawij]
coloured (pencils)	кольоровий	[kolʲo'rɔwij]
colour (e.g. ~ film)	кольоровий	[kolʲo'rɔwij]
black-and-white (adj)	чорно-білий	['ʧɔrno 'bilij]
plain (one-coloured)	однобарвний	[odno'barwnij]
multicoloured (adj)	різнобарвний	[rizno'barwnij]

11. Units of measurement

| weight | вага (ж) | [wa'ɦa] |
| length | довжина (ж) | [dowʒi'na] |

width	ширина (ж)	[ʃiri'na]
height	висота (ж)	[wiso'ta]
depth	глибина (ж)	[ɦlibi'na]
volume	об'єм (ч)	[o'bʔɛm]
area	площа (ж)	['plɔɕa]

gram	грам (ч)	[ɦram]
milligram	міліграм (ч)	[mili'ɦram]
kilogram	кілограм (ч)	[kilo'ɦram]
ton	тонна (ж)	['tɔna]
pound	фунт (ч)	['funt]
ounce	унція (ж)	['untsiʲa]

metre	метр (ч)	[mɛtr]
millimetre	міліметр (ч)	[mili'mɛtr]
centimetre	сантиметр (ч)	[santi'mɛtr]
kilometre	кілометр (ч)	[kilo'mɛtr]
mile	миля (ж)	['miʲla]

inch	дюйм (ч)	[dʲujm]
foot	фут (ч)	[fut]
yard	ярд (ч)	[jard]

| square metre | квадратний метр (ч) | [kwad'ratnij mɛtr] |
| hectare | гектар (ч) | [ɦɛk'tar] |

litre	літр (ч)	[litr]
degree	градус (ч)	['ɦradus]
volt	вольт (ч)	[wolʲt]
ampere	ампер (ч)	[am'pɛr]
horsepower	кінська сила (ж)	['kinsʲka 'sila]

quantity	кількість (ж)	['kilʲkistʲ]
a little bit of ...	небагато ...	[nɛba'ɦato]
half	половина (ж)	[polo'wina]
dozen	дюжина (ж)	['dʲuʒina]
piece (item)	штука (ж)	['ʃtuka]

| size | розмір (ч) | ['rɔzmir] |
| scale (map ~) | масштаб (ч) | [masʃ'tab] |

minimal (adj)	мінімальний	[mini'malʲnij]
the smallest (adj)	найменший	[naj'mɛnʃij]
medium (adj)	середній	[sɛ'rɛdnij]
maximal (adj)	максимальний	[maksi'malʲnij]
the largest (adj)	найбільший	[naj'bilʲʃij]

12. Containers

canning jar (glass ~)	банка (ж)	['banka]
tin, can	банка (ж)	['banka]
bucket	відро (с)	[wid'rɔ]
barrel	бочка (ж)	['bɔʧka]
wash basin (e.g., plastic ~)	таз (ч)	[taz]

tank (100L water ~)	бак (ч)	[bak]
hip flask	фляжка (ж)	['flʲaʒka]
jerrycan	каністра (ж)	[ka'nistra]
tank (e.g., tank car)	цистерна (ж)	[tsis'tɛrna]
mug	кухоль (ч)	['kuholʲ]
cup (of coffee, etc.)	чашка (ж)	['tʃaʃka]
saucer	блюдце (с)	['blʲudtsɛ]
glass (tumbler)	склянка (ж)	['sklʲanka]
wine glass	келих (ч)	['kɛlɨh]
stock pot (soup pot)	каструля (ж)	[kas'trulʲa]
bottle (~ of wine)	пляшка (ж)	['plʲaʃka]
neck (of the bottle, etc.)	шийка (ж)	['ʃɪjka]
carafe (decanter)	карафа (ж)	[ka'rafa]
pitcher	глечик (ч)	['hlɛtʃɨk]
vessel (container)	посудина (ж)	[po'sudɪna]
pot (crock, stoneware ~)	горщик (ч)	['hɔrɕɪk]
vase	ваза (ж)	['waza]
flacon, bottle (perfume ~)	флакон (ч)	[fla'kɔn]
vial, small bottle	пляшечка (ж)	['plʲaʃɛtʃka]
tube (of toothpaste)	тюбик (ч)	['tʲubɪk]
sack (bag)	мішок (ч)	[mi'ʃɔk]
bag (paper ~, plastic ~)	пакет (ч)	[pa'kɛt]
packet (of cigarettes, etc.)	пачка (ж)	['patʃka]
box (e.g. shoebox)	коробка (ж)	[ko'rɔbka]
crate	ящик (ч)	['ʲaɕɪk]
basket	кошик (ч)	['kɔʃɪk]

MAIN VERBS

13.   The most important verbs. Part 1

to advise (vt)	**радити**	['raditi]
to agree (say yes)	**погоджуватися**	[po'ɦɔdʒuwatisʲa]
to answer (vi, vt)	**відповідати**	[widpowi'dati]
to apologize (vi)	**вибачатися**	[wiba'tʃatisʲa]
to arrive (vi)	**приїжджати**	[priji'ʒati]
to ask (~ oneself)	**запитувати**	[za'pituwati]
to ask (~ sb to do sth)	**просити**	[pro'siti]
to be (vi)	**бути**	['buti]
to be afraid	**боятися**	[boʲatisʲa]
to be hungry	**хотіти їсти**	[ho'titi 'jisti]
to be interested in …	**цікавитися**	[tsi'kawitisʲa]
to be needed	**бути потрібним**	['buti po'tribnim]
to be surprised	**дивуватись**	[diwu'watisʲ]
to be thirsty	**хотіти пити**	[ho'titi 'piti]
to begin (vt)	**починати**	[potʃi'nati]
to belong to …	**належати**	[na'lɛʒati]
to boast (vi)	**хвастатися**	['hwastatisʲa]
to break (split into pieces)	**ламати**	[la'mati]
to call (~ for help)	**кликати**	['klikati]
can (v aux)	**могти**	[moɦ'ti]
to catch (vt)	**ловити**	[lo'witi]
to change (vt)	**поміняти**	[pomi'nʲati]
to choose (select)	**вибирати**	[wibi'rati]
to come down (the stairs)	**спускатися**	[spus'katisʲa]
to compare (vt)	**зрівнювати**	['zriwnʲuwati]
to complain (vi, vt)	**скаржитися**	['skarʒitisʲa]
to confuse (mix up)	**помилятися**	[pomi'lʲatisʲa]
to continue (vt)	**продовжувати**	[pro'dɔwʒuwati]
to control (vt)	**контролювати**	[kontrolʲu'wati]
to cook (dinner)	**готувати**	[ɦotu'wati]
to cost (vt)	**коштувати**	['kɔʃtuwati]
to count (add up)	**лічити**	[li'tʃiti]
to count on …	**розраховувати на …**	[rozra'ɦɔwuwatɨ na]
to create (vt)	**створити**	[stwo'riti]
to cry (weep)	**плакати**	['plakati]

14.   The most important verbs. Part 2

to deceive (vi, vt)	**обманювати**	[ob'manʲuwati]
to decorate (tree, street)	**прикрашати**	[prikra'ʃati]

to defend (a country, etc.)	захищати	[zahiˈɕati]
to demand (request firmly)	вимагати	[wimaˈɦati]
to dig (vt)	рити	[ˈriti]

to discuss (vt)	обговорювати	[obɦoˈworˈuwati]
to do (vt)	робити	[roˈbiti]
to doubt (have doubts)	сумніватися	[sumniˈwatisˈa]
to drop (let fall)	упускати	[upusˈkati]
to enter (room, house, etc.)	входити	[ˈwhɔditi]

to exist (vi)	існувати	[isnuˈwati]
to expect (foresee)	передбачити	[pɛrɛdˈbatʃiti]
to explain (vt)	пояснювати	[poˈˈasnˈuwati]
to fall (vi)	падати	[ˈpadati]

to fancy (vt)	подобатися	[poˈdɔbatisˈa]
to find (vt)	знаходити	[znaˈhɔditi]
to finish (vt)	закінчувати	[zaˈkintʃuwati]
to fly (vi)	летіти	[lɛˈtiti]
to follow ... (come after)	іти слідом	[iˈti ˈslidom]

to forget (vi, vt)	забувати	[zabuˈwati]
to forgive (vt)	прощати	[proˈɕati]
to give (vt)	давати	[daˈwati]
to give a hint	натякати	[natˈaˈkati]
to go (on foot)	йти	[jti]

to go for a swim	купатися	[kuˈpatisˈa]
to go out (for dinner, etc.)	виходити	[wiˈhɔditi]
to guess (the answer)	відгадати	[widɦaˈdati]

to have (vt)	мати	[ˈmati]
to have breakfast	снідати	[ˈsnidati]
to have dinner	вечеряти	[wɛˈtʃɛrˈati]
to have lunch	обідати	[oˈbidati]
to hear (vt)	чути	[ˈtʃuti]

to help (vt)	допомагати	[dopomaˈɦati]
to hide (vt)	ховати	[hoˈwati]
to hope (vi, vt)	сподіватися	[spodiˈwatisˈa]
to hunt (vi, vt)	полювати	[polˈuˈwati]
to hurry (vi)	поспішати	[pospiˈʃati]

15. The most important verbs. Part 3

to inform (vt)	інформувати	[informuˈwati]
to insist (vi, vt)	наполягати	[napolˈaˈɦati]
to insult (vt)	ображати	[obraˈʒati]
to invite (vt)	запрошувати	[zaˈprɔʃuwati]
to joke (vi)	жартувати	[ʒartuˈwati]

to keep (vt)	зберігати	[zbɛriˈɦati]
to keep silent, to hush	мовчати	[mowˈtʃati]
to kill (vt)	убивати	[ubiˈwati]

to know (sb)	знати	['znati]
to know (sth)	знати	['znati]
to laugh (vi)	сміятися	[smi'ʲatisʲa]
to liberate (city, etc.)	звільняти	[zwilʲ'nʲati]
to look for … (search)	шукати	[ʃu'kati]
to love (sb)	кохати	[ko'hati]
to make a mistake	помилятися	[pomi'ʲatisʲa]
to manage, to run	керувати	[kɛru'wati]
to mean (signify)	означати	[ozna'tʃati]
to mention (talk about)	згадувати	['zɦaduwati]
to miss (school, etc.)	пропускати	[propus'kati]
to notice (see)	помічати	[pomi'tʃati]
to object (vi, vt)	заперечувати	[zapɛ'rɛtʃuwati]
to observe (see)	спостерігати	[spostɛri'ɦati]
to open (vt)	відчинити	[widtʃi'niti]
to order (meal, etc.)	замовляти	[zamow'lʲati]
to order (mil.)	наказувати	[na'kazuwati]
to own (possess)	володіти	[wolo'diti]
to participate (vi)	брати участь	['brati 'utʃastʲ]
to pay (vi, vt)	платити	[pla'titi]
to permit (vt)	дозволяти	[dozwo'lʲati]
to plan (vt)	планувати	[planu'wati]
to play (children)	грати	['ɦrati]
to pray (vi, vt)	молитися	[mo'litisʲa]
to prefer (vt)	воліти	[wo'liti]
to promise (vt)	обіцяти	[obi'ts'ati]
to pronounce (vt)	вимовляти	[wimow'lʲati]
to propose (vt)	пропонувати	[proponu'wati]
to punish (vt)	покарати	[poka'rati]

16. The most important verbs. Part 4

to read (vi, vt)	читати	[tʃi'tati]
to recommend (vt)	рекомендувати	[rɛkomɛndu'wati]
to refuse (vi, vt)	відмовлятися	[widmow'lʲatisʲa]
to regret (be sorry)	жалкувати	[ʒalku'wati]
to rent (sth from sb)	наймати	[naj'mati]
to repeat (say again)	повторювати	[pow'torʲuwati]
to reserve, to book	резервувати	[rɛzɛrwu'wati]
to run (vi)	бігти	['biɦti]
to save (rescue)	рятувати	[rʲatu'wati]
to say (~ thank you)	сказати	[ska'zati]
to scold (vt)	лаяти	['laʲati]
to see (vt)	бачити	['batʃiti]
to sell (vt)	продавати	[proda'wati]
to send (vt)	відправляти	[widpraw'lʲati]
to shoot (vi)	стріляти	[stri'lʲati]

to shout (vi)	кричати	[kri'ʧati]
to show (vt)	показувати	[po'kazuwati]
to sign (document)	підписувати	[pid'pisuwati]

to sit down (vi)	сідати	[si'dati]
to smile (vi)	посміхатися	[posmi'hatisʲa]
to speak (vi, vt)	розмовляти	[rozmow'lʲati]
to steal (money, etc.)	красти	['krasti]
to stop (for pause, etc.)	зупинятися	[zupi'nʲatisʲa]

to stop (please ~ calling me)	припиняти	[pripi'nʲati]
to study (vt)	вивчати	[wiw'ʧati]
to swim (vi)	плавати	['plawati]
to take (vt)	брати	['brati]
to think (vi, vt)	думати	['dumati]

to threaten (vt)	погрожувати	[poɦ'roʒuwati]
to touch (with hands)	торкати	[tor'kati]
to translate (vt)	перекладати	[pɛrɛkla'dati]
to trust (vt)	довіряти	[dowi'rʲati]
to try (attempt)	пробувати	['probuwati]

to turn (e.g., ~ left)	повертати	[powɛr'tati]
to underestimate (vt)	недооцінювати	[nɛdoo'ʦinʲuwati]
to understand (vt)	розуміти	[rozu'miti]
to unite (vt)	об'єднувати	[o'bʲɛdnuwati]
to wait (vt)	чекати	[ʧɛ'kati]

to want (wish, desire)	хотіти	[ho'titi]
to warn (vt)	попереджувати	[popɛ'rɛʤuwati]
to work (vi)	працювати	[pratsʲu'wati]
to write (vt)	писати	[pi'sati]
to write down	записувати	[za'pisuwati]

TIME. CALENDAR

17. Weekdays

Monday	понеділок (ч)	[ponɛ'dilok]
Tuesday	вівторок (ч)	[wiw'tɔrok]
Wednesday	середа (ж)	[sɛrɛ'da]
Thursday	четвер (ч)	[ʧɛt'wɛr]
Friday	п'ятниця (ж)	['pʲatnʲiʦʲa]
Saturday	субота (ж)	[su'bɔta]
Sunday	неділя (ж)	[nɛ'dilʲa]

today (adv)	сьогодні	[sʲo'ɦɔdni]
tomorrow (adv)	завтра	['zawtra]
the day after tomorrow	післязавтра	[pislʲa'zawtra]
yesterday (adv)	вчора	['wʧɔra]
the day before yesterday	позавчора	[pozaw'ʧɔra]

day	день (ч)	[dɛnʲ]
working day	робочий день (ч)	[ro'bɔʧij dɛnʲ]
public holiday	святковий день (ч)	[swʲat'kɔwij dɛnʲ]
day off	вихідний день (ч)	[wɨhid'nij dɛnʲ]
weekend	вихідні (мн)	[wɨhid'ni]

all day long	весь день	[wɛsʲ dɛnʲ]
the next day (adv)	на наступний день	[na na'stupnij dɛnʲ]
two days ago	2 дні тому	[dwa dni 'tɔmu]
the day before	напередодні	[napɛrɛ'dɔdni]
daily (adj)	щоденний	[ɕo'dɛnij]
every day (adv)	щодня	[ɕod'nʲa]

week	тиждень (ч)	['tiʒdɛnʲ]
last week (adv)	на минулому тижні	[na mɨ'nulomu 'tiʒni]
next week (adv)	на наступному тижні	[na na'stupnomu 'tiʒni]
weekly (adj)	щотижневий	[ɕotiʒ'nɛwij]
every week (adv)	щотижня	[ɕo'tiʒnʲa]
twice a week	два рази на тиждень	[dwa 'razɨ na 'tiʒdɛnʲ]
every Tuesday	кожен вівторок	['kɔʒɛn wiw'tɔrok]

18. Hours. Day and night

morning	ранок (ч)	['ranok]
in the morning	вранці	['wranʦi]
noon, midday	полудень (ч)	['pɔludɛnʲ]
in the afternoon	після обіду	['pislʲa o'bidu]

evening	вечір (ч)	['wɛʧir]
in the evening	увечері	[u'wɛʧɛri]

night	ніч (ж)	[nitʃ]
at night	уночі	[uno'tʃi]
midnight	північ (ж)	['piwnitʃ]

second	секунда (ж)	[sɛ'kunda]
minute	хвилина (ж)	[hwi'lina]
hour	година (ж)	[ɦo'dina]
half an hour	півгодини (мн)	[piwɦo'dini]
a quarter-hour	чверть (ж) години	[tʃwɛrtʲ ɦo'dini]
fifteen minutes	15 хвилин	[pʲat'nadtsʲatʲ hwi'lin]
24 hours	доба (ж)	[do'ba]

sunrise	схід (ч) сонця	[shid 'sɔntsʲa]
dawn	світанок (ч)	[swi'tanok]
early morning	ранній ранок (ч)	['ranij 'ranok]
sunset	захід (ч)	['zahid]

early in the morning	рано вранці	['rano 'wrantsi]
this morning	сьогодні вранці	[sʲo'ɦodni 'wrantsi]
tomorrow morning	завтра вранці	['zawtra 'wrantsi]

this afternoon	сьогодні вдень	[sʲo'ɦodni wdɛnʲ]
in the afternoon	після обіду	['pislʲa o'bidu]
tomorrow afternoon	завтра після обіду (ч)	['zawtra 'pislʲa o'bidu]

| tonight (this evening) | сьогодні увечері | [sʲo'ɦodni u'wɛtʃɛri] |
| tomorrow night | завтра увечері | ['zawtra u'wɛtʃɛri] |

at 3 o'clock sharp	рівно о третій годині	['riwno o t'rɛtij ɦo'dini]
about 4 o'clock	біля четвертої години	['bilʲa tʃɛt'wɛrtoji ɦo'dini]
by 12 o'clock	до дванадцятої години	[do dwa'nadtsʲatoji ɦo'dini]

in 20 minutes	за двадцять хвилин	[za 'dwadtsʲatʲ hwi'lin]
in an hour	за годину	[za ɦo'dinu]
on time (adv)	вчасно	['wtʃasno]

a quarter to …	без чверті	[bɛz 'tʃwɛrti]
within an hour	на протязі години	[na 'protʲazi ɦo'dini]
every 15 minutes	що п'ятнадцять хвилин	[ɕo pʲat'nadtsʲatʲ hwi'lin]
round the clock	цілодобово	[tsilodo'bɔwo]

19. Months. Seasons

January	січень (ч)	['sitʃɛnʲ]
February	лютий (ч)	['lʲutij]
March	березень (ч)	['bɛrɛzɛnʲ]
April	квітень (ч)	['kwitɛnʲ]
May	травень (ч)	['trawɛnʲ]
June	червень (ч)	['tʃɛrwɛnʲ]

July	липень (ч)	['lipɛnʲ]
August	серпень (ч)	['sɛrpɛnʲ]
September	вересень (ч)	['wɛrɛsɛnʲ]
October	жовтень (ч)	['ʒɔwtɛnʲ]

| November | листопад (ч) | [lɪstoˈpad] |
| December | грудень (ч) | [ˈɦrudɛnʲ] |

spring	весна (ж)	[wɛsˈna]
in spring	навесні	[nawɛsˈni]
spring (as adj)	весняний	[wɛsˈnʲanij]

summer	літо (с)	[ˈlito]
in summer	влітку	[ˈwlitku]
summer (as adj)	літній	[ˈlitnij]

autumn	осінь (ж)	[ˈɔsinʲ]
in autumn	восени	[wosɛˈnɪ]
autumn (as adj)	осінній	[oˈsinij]

winter	зима (ж)	[zɪˈma]
in winter	взимку	[ˈwzɪmku]
winter (as adj)	зимовий	[zɪˈmɔwij]

month	місяць (ч)	[ˈmisʲats]
this month	в цьому місяці (ч)	[w tsʲomu ˈmisʲatsi]
next month	в наступному місяці (ч)	[w naˈstupnomu ˈmisʲatsi]
last month	в минулому місяці (ч)	[w mɪˈnulomu ˈmisʲatsi]

a month ago	місяць (ч) тому	[ˈmisʲats toˈmu]
in a month (a month later)	через місяць	[ˈtʃɛrɛz ˈmisʲats]
in 2 months (2 months later)	через 2 місяці	[ˈtʃɛrɛz dwa ˈmisʲatsi]
the whole month	весь місяць (ч)	[wɛsʲ ˈmisʲats]
all month long	цілий місяць	[ˈtsilij ˈmisʲats]

monthly (~ magazine)	щомісячний	[ɕoˈmisʲatʃnij]
monthly (adv)	щомісяця	[ɕoˈmisʲatsʲa]
every month	кожний місяць (ч)	[ˈkɔʒnij ˈmisʲats]
twice a month	два рази на місяць	[dwa ˈrazɪ na ˈmisʲats]

year	рік (ч)	[rik]
this year	в цьому році	[w tsʲomu ˈrɔtsi]
next year	в наступному році	[w naˈstupnomu ˈrɔtsi]
last year	в минулому році	[w mɪˈnulomu ˈrɔtsi]

a year ago	рік тому	[rik ˈtɔmu]
in a year	через рік	[ˈtʃɛrɛz rik]
in two years	через два роки	[ˈtʃɛrɛz dwa ˈrɔki]
the whole year	увесь рік	[uˈwɛsʲ rik]
all year long	цілий рік	[ˈtsilij rik]

every year	кожен рік	[ˈkɔʒɛn ˈrik]
annual (adj)	щорічний	[ɕoˈritʃnij]
annually (adv)	щороку	[ɕoˈrɔku]
4 times a year	чотири рази на рік	[tʃoˈtɪri ˈrazɪ na rik]

date (e.g. today's ~)	число (с)	[tʃɪsˈlɔ]
date (e.g. ~ of birth)	дата (ж)	[ˈdata]
calendar	календар (ч)	[kalɛnˈdar]
half a year	півроку	[piwˈrɔku]
six months	піврічча (с)	[piwˈritʃʲa]

| season (summer, etc.) | **сезон** (ч) | [sɛ'zɔn] |
| century | **вік** (ч) | [wik] |

TRAVEL. HOTEL

20. Trip. Travel

tourism, travel	туризм (ч)	[tu'rizm]
tourist	турист (ч)	[tu'rist]
trip, voyage	мандрівка (ж)	[mand'riwka]
adventure	пригода (ж)	[pri'ɦoda]
trip, journey	поїздка (ж)	[po'jizdka]
holiday	відпустка (ж)	[wid'pustka]
to be on holiday	бути у відпустці	['buti u wid'pusttsi]
rest	відпочинок (ч)	[widpo'tʃinok]
train	поїзд (ч)	['pojizd]
by train	поїздом	['pojizdom]
aeroplane	літак (ч)	[li'tak]
by aeroplane	літаком	[lita'kɔm]
by car	автомобілем	[awtomo'bilɛm]
by ship	кораблем	[korab'lɛm]
luggage	багаж (ч)	[ba'ɦaʒ]
suitcase	валіза (ж)	[wa'liza]
luggage trolley	візок (ч) для багажу	[wi'zɔk dlʲa baɦa'ʒu]
passport	паспорт (ч)	['pasport]
visa	віза (ж)	['wiza]
ticket	квиток (ч)	[kwi'tɔk]
air ticket	авіаквиток (ч)	[awiakwi'tɔk]
guidebook	путівник (ч)	[putiw'nik]
map (tourist ~)	карта (ж)	['karta]
area (rural ~)	місцевість (ж)	[mis'tsɛwistʲ]
place, site	місце (с)	['mistsɛ]
exotica (n)	екзотика (ж)	[ɛk'zɔtika]
exotic (adj)	екзотичний	[ɛkzo'titʃnij]
amazing (adj)	дивовижний	['diwowiʒnij]
group	група (ж)	['ɦrupa]
excursion, sightseeing tour	екскурсія (ж)	[ɛks'kursiʲa]
guide (person)	екскурсовод (ч)	[ɛkskurso'wɔd]

21. Hotel

hotel	готель (ч)	[ɦo'tɛlʲ]
motel	мотель (ч)	[mo'tɛlʲ]
three-star (~ hotel)	три зірки	[trɨ 'zirkɨ]

five-star	п'ять зірок	[pʲatʲ ziˈrɔk]
to stay (in a hotel, etc.)	зупинитися	[zupiˈnitisʲa]
room	номер (ч)	[ˈnɔmɛr]
single room	одномісний номер (ч)	[odnoˈmisnij nomɛr]
double room	двомісний номер (ч)	[dwoˈmisnij ˈnɔmɛr]
to book a room	резервувати номер	[rɛzɛrwuˈwatʲ ˈnɔmɛr]
half board	напівпансіон (ч)	[napiwpansiˈɔn]
full board	повний пансіон (ч)	[ˈpɔwnij pansiˈɔn]
with bath	з ванною	[z ˈwanoʲu]
with shower	з душем	[z ˈduʃɛm]
satellite television	супутникове телебачення (с)	[suˈputnikowɛ tɛlɛˈbatʃɛnʲa]
air-conditioner	кондиціонер (ч)	[kondiʦsioˈnɛr]
towel	рушник (ч)	[ruʃˈnik]
key	ключ (ч)	[klʲutʃ]
administrator	адміністратор (ч)	[adminiˈstrator]
chambermaid	покоївка (ж)	[pokoˈjiwka]
porter	носильник (ч)	[noˈsilʲnik]
doorman	портьє (ч)	[porˈtʲɛ]
restaurant	ресторан (ч)	[rɛstoˈran]
pub, bar	бар (ч)	[bar]
breakfast	сніданок (ч)	[sniˈdanok]
dinner	вечеря (ж)	[wɛˈtʃɛrʲa]
buffet	шведський стіл (ч)	[ˈʃwɛdsʲkij stil]
lobby	вестибюль (ч)	[wɛstiˈbʲulʲ]
lift	ліфт (ч)	[lift]
DO NOT DISTURB	НЕ ТУРБУВАТИ	[nɛ turbuˈwati]
NO SMOKING	ПАЛИТИ ЗАБОРОНЕНО	[paˈliti zaboˈrɔnɛno]

22. Sightseeing

monument	пам'ятник (ч)	[ˈpamʲatnik]
fortress	фортеця (ж)	[forˈtɛʦsʲa]
palace	палац (ч)	[paˈlaʦs]
castle	замок (ч)	[ˈzamok]
tower	вежа (ж)	[ˈwɛʒa]
mausoleum	мавзолей (ч)	[mawzoˈlɛj]
architecture	архітектура (ж)	[arhitɛkˈtura]
medieval (adj)	середньовічний	[sɛrɛdnʲoˈwitʃnij]
ancient (adj)	старовинний	[staroˈwinij]
national (adj)	національний	[naʦsioˈnalʲnij]
famous (monument, etc.)	відомий	[wiˈdɔmij]
tourist	турист (ч)	[tuˈrist]
guide (person)	гід (ч)	[ɦid]
excursion, sightseeing tour	екскурсія (ж)	[ɛksˈkursiʲa]

to show (vt)	показувати	[po'kazuwati]
to tell (vt)	розповідати	[rozpowi'dati]
to find (vt)	знайти	[znaj'ti]
to get lost (lose one's way)	загубитися	[zaɦu'bitisʲa]
map (e.g. underground ~)	схема (ж)	['shɛma]
map (e.g. city ~)	план (ч)	[plan]
souvenir, gift	сувенір (ч)	[suwɛ'nir]
gift shop	магазин (ч) сувенірів	[maɦa'zin suwɛ'niriw]
to take pictures	фотографувати	[fotoɦrafu'wati]
to have one's picture taken	фотографуватися	[fotoɦrafu'watisʲa]

TRANSPORT

23. Airport

airport	**аеропорт** (ч)	[aɛro'pɔrt]
aeroplane	**літак** (ч)	[li'tak]
airline	**авіакомпанія** (ж)	[awiakom'paniʲa]
air traffic controller	**диспетчер** (ч)	[dis'pɛʧɛr]
departure	**виліт** (ч)	['wilit]
arrival	**приліт** (ч)	[pri'lit]
to arrive (by plane)	**прилетіти**	[pri'lɛtiti]
departure time	**час** (ч) **вильоту**	[ʧas 'wilʲotu]
arrival time	**час** (ч) **прильоту**	[ʧas prilʲotu]
to be delayed	**затримуватися**	[za'trimuwatisʲa]
flight delay	**затримка** (ж) **вильоту**	[za'trimka 'wilʲotu]
information board	**інформаційне табло** (с)	[informa'ʦijnɛ tab'lɔ]
information	**інформація** (ж)	[infor'maʦiʲa]
to announce (vt)	**оголошувати**	[oɦo'lɔʃuwati]
flight (e.g. next ~)	**рейс** (ч)	[rɛjs]
customs	**митниця** (ж)	['mitniʦʲa]
customs officer	**митник** (ч)	['mitnik]
customs declaration	**декларація** (ж)	[dɛkla'raʦiʲa]
to fill in (vt)	**заповнити**	[za'powniti]
to fill in the declaration	**заповнити декларацію**	[za'powniti dɛkla'raʦiʲu]
passport control	**паспортний контроль** (ч)	['pasportnij kon'trɔlʲ]
luggage	**багаж** (ч)	[ba'ɦaʒ]
hand luggage	**ручний вантаж** (ж)	[ruʧ'nij wan'taʒ]
luggage trolley	**візок** (ч) **для багажу**	[wi'zɔk dlʲa baɦa'ʒu]
landing	**посадка** (ж)	[po'sadka]
landing strip	**посадкова смуга** (ж)	[po'sadkowa 'smuɦa]
to land (vi)	**сідати**	[si'dati]
airstair (passenger stair)	**трап** (ч)	[trap]
check-in	**реєстрація** (ж)	[rɛɛ'straʦiʲa]
check-in counter	**реєстрація** (ж)	[rɛɛ'straʦiʲa]
to check-in (vi)	**зареєструватися**	[zarɛɛstru'watisʲa]
boarding card	**посадковий талон** (ч)	[po'sadkowij ta'lɔn]
departure gate	**вихід** (ч)	['wihid]
transit	**транзит** (ч)	[tran'zit]
to wait (vt)	**чекати**	[ʧɛ'kati]
departure lounge	**зал** (ч) **очікування**	['zal o'ʧikuwanʲa]

| to see off | проводжати | [prowo'dʒati] |
| to say goodbye | прощатися | [pro'çatisʲa] |

24. Aeroplane

aeroplane	літак (ч)	[li'tak]
air ticket	авіаквиток (ч)	[awiakwɨ'tɔk]
airline	авіакомпанія (ж)	[awiakom'paniʲa]
airport	аеропорт (ч)	[aɛro'pɔrt]
supersonic (adj)	надзвуковий	[nadzwuko'wɨj]

captain	командир (ч) корабля	[koman'dir korab'lʲa]
crew	екіпаж (ч)	[ɛki'paʒ]
pilot	пілот (ч)	[pi'lɔt]
stewardess	стюардеса (ж)	[stʲuar'dɛsa]
navigator	штурман (ч)	['ʃturman]

wings	крила (мн)	['krila]
tail	хвіст (ч)	[hwist]
cockpit	кабіна (ж)	[ka'bina]
engine	двигун (ч)	[dwɨ'ɦun]
undercarriage (landing gear)	шасі (с)	[ʃa'si]
turbine	турбіна (ж)	[tur'bina]
propeller	пропелер (ч)	[pro'pɛlɛr]
black box	чорна скринька (ж)	['tʃorna 'skrinʲka]
yoke (control column)	штурвал (ч)	[ʃtur'wal]
fuel	пальне (с)	[palʲ'nɛ]

safety card	інструкція (ж)	[inst'ruktsiʲa]
oxygen mask	киснева маска (ж)	['kisnɛwa 'maska]
uniform	уніформа (ж)	[uni'forma]
lifejacket	рятувальний жилет (ч)	[rʲatu'walʲnij ʒi'lɛt]
parachute	парашут (ч)	[para'ʃut]
takeoff	зліт (ч)	[zlit]
to take off (vi)	злітати	[zli'tati]
runway	злітна смуга (ж)	['zlitna 'smuɦa]

visibility	видимість (ж)	['widimistʲ]
flight (act of flying)	політ (ч)	[po'lit]
altitude	висота (ж)	[wiso'ta]
air pocket	повітряна яма (ж)	[po'witrʲana 'jama]

seat	місце (с)	['mistsɛ]
headphones	навушники (мн)	[na'wuʃniki]
folding tray (tray table)	відкидний столик (ч)	[widkid'nij 'stɔlik]
airplane window	ілюмінатор (ч)	[ilʲumi'nator]
aisle	прохід (ч)	[pro'hid]

25. Train

| train | поїзд (ч) | ['pojizd] |
| commuter train | електропоїзд (ч) | [ɛlɛktro'pojizd] |

express train	швидкий поїзд (ч)	[ʃwid'kij 'pojizd]
diesel locomotive	тепловоз (ч)	[tɛplo'wɔz]
steam locomotive	паровоз (ч)	[paro'wɔz]
coach, carriage	вагон (ч)	[wa'hɔn]
buffet car	вагон-ресторан (ч)	[wa'hɔn rɛsto'ran]
rails	рейки (мн)	['rɛjki]
railway	залізниця (ж)	[zaliz'nitsʲa]
sleeper (track support)	шпала (ж)	['ʃpala]
platform (railway ~)	платформа (ж)	[plat'fɔrma]
platform (~ 1, 2, etc.)	колія (ж)	['kɔliʲa]
semaphore	семафор (ч)	[sɛma'fɔr]
station	станція (ж)	['stantsiʲa]
train driver	машиніст (ч)	[maʃi'nist]
porter (of luggage)	носильник (ч)	[no'silʲnik]
carriage attendant	провідник (ч)	[prowid'nik]
passenger	пасажир (ч)	[pasa'ʒir]
ticket inspector	контролер (ч)	[kontro'lɛr]
corridor (in train)	коридор (ч)	[kori'dɔr]
emergency brake	стоп-кран (ч)	[stop kran]
compartment	купе (с)	[ku'pɛ]
berth	полиця (ж)	[po'litsʲa]
upper berth	полиця (ж) верхня	[po'litsʲa 'wɛrhnʲa]
lower berth	полиця (ж) нижня	[po'litsʲa 'niʒnʲa]
bed linen, bedding	білизна (ж)	[bi'lizna]
ticket	квиток (ч)	[kwi'tɔk]
timetable	розклад (ч)	['rɔzklad]
information display	табло (с)	[tab'lɔ]
to leave, to depart	відходити	[wid'hɔditi]
departure (of a train)	відправлення (с)	[wid'prawlɛnʲa]
to arrive (ab. train)	прибувати	[pribu'wati]
arrival	прибуття (с)	[pribut'tʲa]
to arrive by train	приїхати поїздом	[pri'jihati 'pojizdom]
to get on the train	сісти на поїзд	['sisti na 'pojizd]
to get off the train	зійти з поїзду	[zij'ti z 'pojizdu]
train crash	катастрофа (ж)	[kata'strɔfa]
steam locomotive	паровоз (ч)	[paro'wɔz]
stoker, fireman	кочегар (ч)	[kotʃɛ'har]
firebox	топка (ж)	['tɔpka]
coal	вугілля (с)	[wu'hilʲa]

26. Ship

ship	корабель (ч)	[kora'bɛlʲ]
vessel	судно (с)	['sudno]

steamship	пароплав (ч)	[paro'plaw]
riverboat	теплохід (ч)	[tɛplo'hid]
cruise ship	лайнер (ч)	['lajnɛr]
cruiser	крейсер (ч)	['krɛjsɛr]
yacht	яхта (ж)	[ˈ'ahta]
tugboat	буксир (ч)	[buk'sir]
barge	баржа (ж)	['barʒa]
ferry	паром (ч)	[pa'rɔm]
sailing ship	вітрильник (ч)	[wi'trilʲnik]
brigantine	бригантина (ж)	[briɦan'tina]
ice breaker	криголам (ч)	[kriɦo'lam]
submarine	човен (ч) підводний	['ʧowɛn pid'wɔdnij]
boat (flat-bottomed ~)	човен (ч)	['ʧowɛn]
dinghy (lifeboat)	шлюпка (ж)	['ʃlʲupka]
lifeboat	шлюпка (ж) рятувальна	['ʃlʲupka rʲatu'walʲna]
motorboat	катер (ч)	['katɛr]
captain	капітан (ч)	[kapi'tan]
seaman	матрос (ч)	[mat'rɔs]
sailor	моряк (ч)	[mo'rʲak]
crew	екіпаж (ч)	[ɛki'paʒ]
boatswain	боцман (ч)	['bɔʦman]
ship's boy	юнга (ч)	['ʲunɦa]
cook	кок (ч)	[kok]
ship's doctor	судновий лікар (ч)	['sudnowij 'likar]
deck	палуба (ж)	['paluba]
mast	щогла (ж)	['ɕoɦla]
sail	вітрило (с)	[wi'trilo]
hold	трюм (ч)	[trʲum]
bow (prow)	ніс (ч)	[nis]
stern	корма (ж)	[kor'ma]
oar	весло (с)	[wɛs'lɔ]
screw propeller	гвинт (ч)	[ɦwint]
cabin	каюта (ж)	[ka'ʲuta]
wardroom	кают-компанія (ж)	[ka'ʲut kom'paniʲa]
engine room	машинне відділення (с)	[ma'ʃinɛ wid'dilɛnʲa]
bridge	капітанський місток (ч)	[kapi'tansʲkij mis'tɔk]
radio room	радіорубка (ж)	[radio'rubka]
wave (radio)	хвиля (ж)	['ɦwilʲa]
logbook	судновий журнал (ч)	['sudnowij ʒur'nal]
spyglass	підзорна труба (ж)	[pi'dzorna tru'ba]
bell	дзвін (ч)	[dzwin]
flag	прапор (ч)	['prapor]
hawser (mooring ~)	канат (ч)	[ka'nat]
knot (bowline, etc.)	вузол (ч)	['wuzol]
deckrails	поручень (ч)	['pɔruʧɛnʲ]

gangway	**трап** (ч)	[trap]
anchor	**якір** (ч)	[ˈʲakir]
to weigh anchor	**підняти якір**	[pidˈnʲatɨ ˈjakir]
to drop anchor	**кинути якір**	[ˈkɨnutɨ ˈjakir]
anchor chain	**якірний ланцюг** (ч)	[ˈʲakirnɨj lanˈʦʲuɦ]
port (harbour)	**порт** (ч)	[port]
quay, wharf	**причал** (ч)	[prɨˈʧal]
to berth (moor)	**причалювати**	[prɨˈʧalʲuwatɨ]
to cast off	**відчалювати**	[widˈʧalʲuwatɨ]
trip, voyage	**подорож** (ж)	[ˈpɔdorɔʒ]
cruise (sea trip)	**круїз** (ч)	[kruˈjiz]
course (route)	**курс** (ч)	[kurs]
route (itinerary)	**маршрут** (ч)	[marˈʃrut]
fairway (safe water channel)	**фарватер** (ч)	[farˈwatɛr]
shallows	**мілина** (ж)	[miliˈna]
to run aground	**сісти на мілину**	[ˈsistɨ na miliˈnu]
storm	**буря** (ж)	[ˈburʲa]
signal	**сигнал** (ч)	[sɨɦˈnal]
to sink (vi)	**тонути**	[toˈnutɨ]
SOS (distress signal)	**SOS**	[sos]
ring buoy	**рятувальний круг** (ч)	[rʲatuˈwalʲnɨj ˈkruɦ]

CITY

27. Urban transport

bus, coach	автобус (ч)	[aw'tɔbus]
tram	трамвай (ч)	[tram'waj]
trolleybus	тролейбус (ч)	[tro'lɛjbus]
route (bus ~)	маршрут (ч)	[marʃrut]
number (e.g. bus ~)	номер (ч)	['nɔmɛr]
to go by ...	їхати на ...	['jihati na]
to get on (~ the bus)	сісти	['sisti]
to get off ...	зійти	[zij'ti]
stop (e.g. bus ~)	зупинка (ж)	[zu'pinka]
next stop	наступна зупинка (ж)	[na'stupna zu'pinka]
terminus	кінцева зупинка (ж)	[kin'tsɛwa zu'pinka]
timetable	розклад (ч)	['rɔzklad]
to wait (vt)	чекати	[tʃɛ'kati]
ticket	квиток (ч)	[kwi'tɔk]
fare	вартість (ж) квитка	['wartistʲ kwit'ka]
cashier (ticket seller)	касир (ч)	[ka'sir]
ticket inspection	контроль (ч)	[kon'trɔlʲ]
ticket inspector	контролер (ч)	[kontro'lɛr]
to be late (for ...)	запізнюватися	[za'piznʲuwatisʲa]
to miss (~ the train, etc.)	спізнитися	[spiz'nitisʲa]
to be in a hurry	поспішати	[pospi'ʃati]
taxi, cab	таксі (с)	[tak'si]
taxi driver	таксист (ч)	[tak'sist]
by taxi	на таксі	[na tak'si]
taxi rank	стоянка (с) таксі	[sto'ʲanka tak'si]
to call a taxi	викликати таксі	['wiklikati tak'si]
to take a taxi	взяти таксі	['wzʲati tak'si]
traffic	вуличний рух (ч)	['wulitʃnij ruh]
traffic jam	пробка (ж)	['prɔbka]
rush hour	години (мн) пік	[ɦo'dini pik]
to park (vi)	паркуватися	[parku'watisʲa]
to park (vt)	паркувати	[parku'wati]
car park	стоянка (ж)	[sto'ʲanka]
underground, tube	метро (с)	[mɛt'rɔ]
station	станція (ж)	['stantsiʲa]
to take the tube	їхати в метро	['jihati w mɛt'rɔ]
train	поїзд (ч)	['pɔjizd]
train station	вокзал (ч)	[wok'zal]

28. City. Life in the city

city, town	місто (с)	['misto]
capital city	столиця (ж)	[sto'liʦʲa]
village	село (с)	[sɛ'lɔ]
city map	план (ч) міста	[plan 'mista]
city centre	центр (ч) міста	[ʦɛntr 'mista]
suburb	передмістя (с)	[pɛrɛd'mistʲa]
suburban (adj)	приміський	[primisʲʲkij]
outskirts	околиця (ж)	[o'kɔliʦʲa]
environs (suburbs)	околиці (мн)	[o'kɔliʦi]
city block	квартал (ч)	[kwar'tal]
residential block (area)	житловий квартал (ч)	[ʒitlo'wij kwar'tal]
traffic	рух (ч)	[ruh]
traffic lights	світлофор (ч)	[switlo'for]
public transport	міський транспорт (ч)	[misʲʲkij 'transport]
crossroads	перехрестя (с)	[pɛrɛh'rɛstʲa]
zebra crossing	перехід (ч)	[pɛrɛ'hid]
pedestrian subway	підземний перехід (ч)	[pi'dzɛmnij pɛrɛ'hid]
to cross (~ the street)	переходити	[pɛrɛ'hɔditi]
pedestrian	пішохід (ч)	[piʃo'hid]
pavement	тротуар (ч)	[trotu'ar]
bridge	міст (ч)	[mist]
embankment (river walk)	набережна (ж)	['nabɛrɛʒna]
fountain	фонтан (ч)	[fon'tan]
allée (garden walkway)	алея (ж)	[a'lɛʲa]
park	парк (ч)	[park]
boulevard	бульвар (ч)	[bulʲʲwar]
square	площа (ж)	['plɔɕa]
avenue (wide street)	проспект (ч)	[pros'pɛkt]
street	вулиця (ж)	['wuliʦʲa]
side street	провулок (ч)	[pro'wulok]
dead end	глухий кут (ч)	[ɦlu'hij kut]
house	будинок (ч)	[bu'dinok]
building	споруда (ж)	[spo'ruda]
skyscraper	хмарочос (ч)	[hmaro'ʧɔs]
facade	фасад (ч)	[fa'sad]
roof	дах (ч)	[dah]
window	вікно (с)	[wik'nɔ]
arch	арка (ж)	['arka]
column	колона (ж)	[ko'lɔna]
corner	ріг (ч)	[riɦ]
shop window	вітрина (ж)	[wi'trina]
signboard (store sign, etc.)	вивіска (ж)	['wiwiska]
poster (e.g., playbill)	афіша (ж)	[a'fiʃa]
advertising poster	рекламний плакат (ч)	[rɛk'lamnij pla'kat]

hoarding	рекламний щит (ч)	[rɛk'lamnij çit]
rubbish	сміття (с)	[smit't'a]
rubbish bin	урна (ж)	['urna]
to litter (vi)	смітити	[smi'titi]
rubbish dump	смітник (ч)	[smit'nik]

telephone box	телефонна будка (ж)	[tɛlɛ'fona 'budka]
lamppost	ліхтарний стовп (ч)	[lih'tarnij stowp]
bench (park ~)	лавка (ж)	['lawka]

police officer	поліцейський (ч)	[poli'tsɛjs'kij]
police	поліція (ж)	[po'litsi'a]
beggar	жебрак (ч)	[ʒɛb'rak]
homeless (n)	безпритульний (ч)	[bɛzpri'tul'nij]

29. Urban institutions

shop	магазин (ч)	[maɦa'zin]
chemist, pharmacy	аптека (ж)	[ap'tɛka]
optician (spectacles shop)	оптика (ж)	['ɔptika]
shopping centre	торгівельний центр (ч)	[torɦi'wɛl'nij 'tsɛntr]
supermarket	супермаркет (ч)	[supɛr'markɛt]

bakery	булочна (ж)	['bulotʃna]
baker	пекар (ч)	['pɛkar]
cake shop	кондитерська (ж)	[kon'ditɛrs'ka]
grocery shop	бакалія (ж)	[baka'li'a]
butcher shop	м'ясний магазин (ч)	[m'ʲas'nij maɦa'zin]

| greengrocer | овочевий магазин (ч) | [owo'tʃɛwij maɦa'zin] |
| market | ринок (ч) | ['rinok] |

coffee bar	кав'ярня (ж)	[ka'w'ʲarn'ʲa]
restaurant	ресторан (ч)	[rɛsto'ran]
pub, bar	пивна (ж)	[piw'na]
pizzeria	піцерія (ж)	[pitsɛ'ri'a]

hairdresser	перукарня (ж)	[pɛru'karn'ʲa]
post office	пошта (ж)	['pɔʃta]
dry cleaners	хімчистка (ж)	[him'tʃistka]
photo studio	фотоательє (с)	[fotoatɛ'ljɛ]

shoe shop	взуттєвий магазин (ч)	[wzut'tɛwij maɦa'zin]
bookshop	книгарня (ж)	[kni'ɦarn'ʲa]
sports shop	спортивний магазин (ч)	[spor'tiwnij maɦa'zin]

clothes repair shop	ремонт (ч) одягу	[rɛ'mɔnt 'ɔd'aɦu]
formal wear hire	прокат (ч) одягу	[pro'kat 'ɔd'aɦu]
video rental shop	прокат (ч) фільмів	[pro'kat 'fil'miw]

circus	цирк (ч)	[tsirk]
zoo	зоопарк (ч)	[zoo'park]
cinema	кінотеатр (ч)	[kinotɛ'atr]
museum	музей (ч)	[mu'zɛj]

library	бібліотека (ж)	[biblio'tɛka]
theatre	театр (ч)	[tɛ'atr]
opera (opera house)	опера (ж)	['ɔpɛra]
nightclub	нічний клуб (ч)	[nitʃ'nij klub]
casino	казино (с)	[kazi'nɔ]
mosque	мечеть (ж)	[mɛ'tʃɛtʲ]
synagogue	синагога (ж)	[sina'ɦɔɦa]
cathedral	собор (ч)	[so'bɔr]
temple	храм (ч)	[hram]
church	церква (ж)	['tsɛrkwa]
college	інститут (ч)	[insti'tut]
university	університет (ч)	[uniwɛrsi'tɛt]
school	школа (ж)	['ʃkɔla]
prefecture	префектура (ж)	[prɛfɛk'tura]
town hall	мерія (ж)	['mɛriʲa]
hotel	готель (ч)	[ɦo'tɛlʲ]
bank	банк (ч)	[bank]
embassy	посольство (с)	[po'sɔlʲstwo]
travel agency	турагентство (с)	[tura'ɦɛntstwo]
information office	довідкове бюро (с)	[dowid'kɔwɛ bʲu'rɔ]
currency exchange	обмінний пункт (ч)	[ob'minij punkt]
underground, tube	метро (с)	[mɛt'rɔ]
hospital	лікарня (ж)	[li'karnʲa]
petrol station	бензоколонка (ж)	[bɛnzoko'lɔnka]
car park	стоянка (ж)	[sto'ʲanka]

30. Signs

signboard (store sign, etc.)	вивіска (ж)	['wiwiska]
notice (door sign, etc.)	напис (ч)	['napis]
poster	плакат (ч)	[pla'kat]
direction sign	дороговказ (ч)	[doroɦow'kaz]
arrow (sign)	стрілка (ж)	['strilka]
caution	застереження (с)	[zastɛ'rɛʒɛnʲa]
warning sign	попередження (с)	[popɛ'rɛdʒɛnʲa]
to warn (vt)	попереджувати	[popɛ'rɛdʒuwati]
rest day (weekly ~)	вихідний день (ч)	[wihid'nij dɛnʲ]
timetable (schedule)	розклад (ч)	['rɔzklad]
opening hours	години (мн) роботи	[ɦo'dini ro'bɔti]
WELCOME!	ЛАСКАВО ПРОСИМО!	[las'kawo 'prɔsimo]
ENTRANCE	ВХІД	[whid]
WAY OUT	ВИХІД	['wihid]
PUSH	ВІД СЕБЕ	[wid 'sɛbɛ]
PULL	ДО СЕБЕ	[do 'sɛbɛ]

| OPEN | ВІДЧИНЕНО | [wid'ʧinɛno] |
| CLOSED | ЗАЧИНЕНО | [za'ʧinɛno] |

| WOMEN | ДЛЯ ЖІНОК | [dlʲa ʒi'nɔk] |
| MEN | ДЛЯ ЧОЛОВІКІВ | [dlʲa ʧolowi'kiw] |

DISCOUNTS	ЗНИЖКИ	['zniʒki]
SALE	РОЗПРОДАЖ	[rozp'rɔdaʒ]
NEW!	НОВИНКА!	[no'winka]
FREE	БЕЗКОШТОВНО	[bɛzkoʃ'towno]

ATTENTION!	УВАГА!	[u'waɦa]
NO VACANCIES	МІСЦЬ НЕМАЄ	[mists nɛ'maɛ]
RESERVED	ЗАРЕЗЕРВОВАНО	[zarɛzɛr'wɔwano]

| ADMINISTRATION | АДМІНІСТРАЦІЯ | [admini'stratsiʲa] |
| STAFF ONLY | ТІЛЬКИ ДЛЯ ПЕРСОНАЛУ | ['tilʲki dlʲa pɛrso'nalu] |

BEWARE OF THE DOG!	ОБЕРЕЖНО! ЗЛИЙ ПЕС	[obɛ'rɛʒno! zlij pɛs]
NO SMOKING	ПАЛИТИ ЗАБОРОНЕНО	[pa'liti zabo'rɔnɛno]
DO NOT TOUCH!	НЕ ТОРКАТИСЯ!	[nɛ tor'katisʲa]

DANGEROUS	НЕБЕЗПЕЧНО	[nɛbɛz'pɛʧno]
DANGER	НЕБЕЗПЕКА	[nɛbɛz'pɛka]
HIGH VOLTAGE	ВИСОКА НАПРУГА	[wi'sɔka na'pruɦa]
NO SWIMMING!	КУПАТИСЯ ЗАБОРОНЕНО	[ku'patisʲa zabo'rɔnɛno]
OUT OF ORDER	НЕ ПРАЦЮЄ	[nɛ pra'tsʲuɛ]

FLAMMABLE	ВОГНЕНЕБЕЗПЕЧНО	[woɦnɛnɛbɛz'pɛʧno]
FORBIDDEN	ЗАБОРОНЕНО	[zabo'rɔnɛno]
NO TRESPASSING!	ПРОХІД ЗАБОРОНЕНО	[pro'hid zabo'rɔnɛno]
WET PAINT	ПОФАРБОВАНО	[pofar'bɔwano]

31. Shopping

to buy (purchase)	купляти	[kup'lʲati]
shopping	покупка (ж)	[po'kupka]
to go shopping	робити покупки	[ro'biti po'kupki]
shopping	шопінг (ч)	['ʃopinɦ]

| to be open (ab. shop) | працювати | [pratsʲu'wati] |
| to be closed | зачинитися | [zaʧi'nitisʲa] |

footwear, shoes	взуття (с)	[wzut'tʲa]
clothes, clothing	одяг (ч)	['ɔdʲaɦ]
cosmetics	косметика (ж)	[kos'mɛtika]
food products	продукти (мн)	[pro'dukti]
gift, present	подарунок (ч)	[poda'runok]

| shop assistant (masc.) | продавець (ч) | [proda'wɛts] |
| shop assistant (fem.) | продавщиця (ж) | [prodaw'ɕitsʲa] |

| cash desk | каса (ж) | ['kasa] |
| mirror | дзеркало (с) | ['dzɛrkalo] |

counter (shop ~)	прилавок (ч)	[pri'lawok]
fitting room	примірочна (ж)	[pri'mirotʃna]
to try on	приміряти	[pri'mirʲati]
to fit (ab. dress, etc.)	пасувати	[pasu'wati]
to fancy (vt)	подобатися	[po'dɔbatisʲa]
price	ціна (ж)	[ʦi'na]
price tag	цінник (ч)	['ʦinɨk]
to cost (vt)	коштувати	['kɔʃtuwati]
How much?	Скільки?	['skilʲkɨ]
discount	знижка (ж)	['znɨʒka]
inexpensive (adj)	недорогий	[nɛdoro'ɦij]
cheap (adj)	дешевий	[dɛ'ʃɛwij]
expensive (adj)	дорогий	[doro'ɦij]
It's expensive	Це дорого.	[ʦɛ 'dɔroɦo]
hire (n)	прокат (ч)	[pro'kat]
to hire (~ a dinner jacket)	взяти напрокат	['wzʲati napro'kat]
credit (trade credit)	кредит (ч)	[krɛ'dit]
on credit (adv)	в кредит (ч)	[w krɛ'dit]

CLOTHING & ACCESSORIES

32. Outerwear. Coats

clothes	одяг (ч)	['ɔdʲaɦ]
outerwear	верхній одяг (ч)	['wɛrhnij 'ɔdʲaɦ]
winter clothing	зимовий одяг (ч)	[zi'mɔwij 'ɔdʲaɦ]
coat (overcoat)	пальто (с)	[palʲ'tɔ]
fur coat	шуба (ж)	['ʃuba]
fur jacket	кожушок (ч)	[koʒu'ʃɔk]
down coat	пуховик (ч)	[puho'wik]
jacket (e.g. leather ~)	куртка (ж)	['kurtka]
raincoat (trenchcoat, etc.)	плащ (ч)	[plaɕ]
waterproof (adj)	непромокальний	[nɛpromo'kalʲnij]

33. Men's & women's clothing

shirt (button shirt)	сорочка (ж)	[so'rɔtʃka]
trousers	штани (мн)	[ʃta'ni]
jeans	джинси (мн)	['dʒinsi]
suit jacket	піджак (ч)	[pi'dʒak]
suit	костюм (ч)	[kos'tʲum]
dress (frock)	сукня (ж)	['suknʲa]
skirt	спідниця (ж)	[spid'nitsʲa]
blouse	блузка (ж)	['bluzka]
knitted jacket (cardigan, etc.)	кофта (ж)	['kɔfta]
jacket (of a woman's suit)	жакет (ч)	[ʒa'kɛt]
T-shirt	футболка (ж)	[fut'bɔlka]
shorts (short trousers)	шорти (мн)	['ʃɔrti]
tracksuit	спортивний костюм (ч)	[spor'tiwnij kos'tʲum]
bathrobe	халат (ч)	[ha'lat]
pyjamas	піжама (ж)	[pi'ʒama]
jumper (sweater)	светр (ч)	[swɛtr]
pullover	пуловер (ч)	[pulo'wɛr]
waistcoat	жилет (ч)	[ʒi'lɛt]
tailcoat	фрак (ч)	[frak]
dinner suit	смокінг (ч)	['smɔkinɦ]
uniform	форма (ж)	['fɔrma]
workwear	робочий одяг (ж)	[ro'bɔtʃij 'ɔdʲaɦ]
boiler suit	комбінезон (ч)	[kombinɛ'zɔn]
coat (e.g. doctor's smock)	халат (ч)	[ha'lat]

34. Clothing. Underwear

underwear	білизна (ж)	[bi'lizna]
vest (singlet)	майка (ж)	['majka]
socks	шкарпетки (мн)	[ʃkar'pɛtki]
nightdress	нічна сорочка (ж)	[niʧ'na so'rɔʧka]
bra	бюстгальтер (ч)	[bʲust'halʲtɛr]
knee highs (knee-high socks)	гольфи (мн)	['hɔlʲfi]
tights	колготки (мн)	[kol'hɔtki]
stockings (hold ups)	панчохи (мн)	[pan'ʧɔhi]
swimsuit, bikini	купальник (ч)	[ku'palʲnik]

35. Headwear

hat	шапка (ж)	['ʃapka]
trilby hat	капелюх (ч)	[kapɛ'lʲuh]
baseball cap	бейсболка (ж)	[bɛjs'bɔlka]
flatcap	кашкет (ч)	[kaʃ'kɛt]
beret	берет (ч)	[bɛ'rɛt]
hood	каптур (ч)	[kap'tur]
panama hat	панамка (ж)	[pa'namka]
knit cap (knitted hat)	в'язана шапочка (ж)	['wʲazana 'ʃapoʧka]
headscarf	хустка (ж)	['hustka]
women's hat	капелюшок (ч)	[kapɛ'lʲuʃok]
hard hat	каска (ж)	['kaska]
forage cap	пілотка (ж)	[pi'lɔtka]
helmet	шолом (ч)	[ʃo'lɔm]
bowler	котелок (ч)	[kotɛ'lɔk]
top hat	циліндр (ч)	[tsi'lindr]

36. Footwear

footwear	взуття (с)	[wzut'tʲa]
shoes (men's shoes)	черевики (мн)	[ʧɛrɛ'wiki]
shoes (women's shoes)	туфлі (мн)	['tufli]
boots (e.g., cowboy ~)	чоботи (мн)	['ʧɔboti]
carpet slippers	капці (мн)	['kaptsi]
trainers	кросівки (мн)	[kro'siwki]
trainers	кеди (мн)	['kɛdi]
sandals	сандалі (мн)	[san'dali]
cobbler (shoe repairer)	чоботар (ч)	[ʧobo'tar]
heel	каблук (ч)	[kab'luk]
pair (of shoes)	пара (ж)	['para]
lace (shoelace)	шнурок (ч)	[ʃnu'rɔk]

to lace up (vt)	шнурувати	[ʃnuru'wati]
shoehorn	ложка (ж)	['lɔʒka]
shoe polish	крем (ч) для взуття	[krɛm dlʲa wzut'tʲa]

37. Personal accessories

gloves	рукавички (мн)	[ruka'witʃki]
mittens	рукавиці (мн)	[ruka'witsi]
scarf (muffler)	шарф (ч)	[ʃarf]

glasses	окуляри (мн)	[oku'lʲari]
frame (eyeglass ~)	оправа (ж)	[op'rawa]
umbrella	парасолька (ж)	[para'sɔlʲka]
walking stick	ціпок (ч)	[tsi'pɔk]
hairbrush	щітка (ж) для волосся	['ɕitka dlʲa wo'lɔssʲa]
fan	віяло (с)	['wiʲalo]

tie (necktie)	краватка (ж)	[kra'watka]
bow tie	краватка-метелик (ж)	[kra'watka mɛ'tɛlik]
braces	шлейки (мн)	['ʃlɛjki]
handkerchief	носовичок (ч)	[nosowi'tʃɔk]

comb	гребінець (ч)	[ɦrɛbi'nɛts]
hair slide	заколка (ж)	[za'kɔlka]
hairpin	шпилька (ж)	['ʃpilʲka]
buckle	пряжка (ж)	['prʲaʒka]

| belt | пасок (ч) | ['pasok] |
| shoulder strap | ремінь (ч) | ['rɛminʲ] |

bag (handbag)	сумка (ж)	['sumka]
handbag	сумочка (ж)	['sumotʃka]
rucksack	рюкзак (ч)	[rʲuk'zak]

38. Clothing. Miscellaneous

fashion	мода (ж)	['mɔda]
in vogue (adj)	модний	['mɔdnij]
fashion designer	модельєр (ч)	[modɛ'lʲɛr]

collar	комір (ч)	['kɔmir]
pocket	кишеня (ж)	[ki'ʃɛnʲa]
pocket (as adj)	кишеньковий	[kiʃɛnʲ'kɔwij]
sleeve	рукав (ч)	[ru'kaw]
hanging loop	петелька (ж)	[pɛ'tɛlʲka]
flies (on trousers)	ширінка (ж)	[ʃi'rinka]

zip (fastener)	змійка (ж)	['zmijka]
fastener	застібка (ж)	['zastibka]
button	ґудзик (ч)	['gudzik]
buttonhole	петля (ж)	[pɛt'lʲa]
to come off (ab. button)	відірватися	[widir'watisʲa]

to sew (vi, vt)	шити	['ʃiti]
to embroider (vi, vt)	вишивати	[wiʃi'wati]
embroidery	вишивка (ж)	['wiʃiwka]
sewing needle	голка (ж)	['ɦolka]
thread	нитка (ж)	['nitka]
seam	шов (ч)	[ʃow]

to get dirty (vi)	забруднитися	[zabrud'nitisʲa]
stain (mark, spot)	пляма (ж)	['plʲama]
to crease, to crumple	пом'ятися	[po'mʲatisʲa]
to tear, to rip (vt)	порвати	[por'wati]
clothes moth	міль (ж)	[milʲ]

39. Personal care. Cosmetics

toothpaste	зубна паста (ж)	[zub'na 'pasta]
toothbrush	зубна щітка (ж)	[zub'na 'çitka]
to clean one's teeth	чистити зуби	['tʃistiti 'zubi]

razor	бритва (ж)	['britwa]
shaving cream	крем (ч) для гоління	[krɛm dlʲa ɦo'linʲa]
to shave (vi)	голитися	[ɦo'litisʲa]

soap	мило (с)	['milo]
shampoo	шампунь (ч)	[ʃam'punʲ]

scissors	ножиці (мн)	['nɔʒitsi]
nail file	пилочка (ж) для нігтів	['pilotʃka dlʲa 'niɦtiw]
nail clippers	щипчики (мн)	['çiptʃiki]
tweezers	пінцет (ч)	[pin'tsɛt]

cosmetics	косметика (ж)	[kos'mɛtika]
face mask	маска (ж)	['maska]
manicure	манікюр (ч)	[mani'kʲur]
to have a manicure	робити манікюр	[ro'biti mani'kʲur]
pedicure	педикюр (ч)	[pɛdi'kʲur]

make-up bag	косметичка (ж)	[kosmɛ'titʃka]
face powder	пудра (ж)	['pudra]
powder compact	пудрениця (ж)	['pudrɛnitsʲa]
blusher	рум'яна (мн)	[ru'mʲana]

perfume (bottled)	парфуми (мн)	[par'fumi]
toilet water (lotion)	туалетна вода (ж)	[tua'lɛtna wo'da]
lotion	лосьйон (ч)	[lo'sjon]
cologne	одеколон (ч)	[odɛko'lɔn]

eyeshadow	тіні (мн) для повік	['tini dlʲa po'wik]
eyeliner	олівець (ч) для очей	[oli'wɛts dlʲa o'tʃɛj]
mascara	туш (ж)	[tuʃ]

lipstick	губна помада (ж)	[ɦub'na po'mada]
nail polish	лак (ч) для нігтів	[lak dlʲa 'niɦtiw]
hair spray	лак (ч) для волосся	[lak dlʲa wo'lɔssʲa]

deodorant	дезодорант (ч)	[dɛzodoˈrant]
cream	крем (ч)	[krɛm]
face cream	крем (ч) для обличчя	[krɛm dlʲa obˈlitʃʲa]
hand cream	крем (ч) для рук	[krɛm dlʲa ruk]
anti-wrinkle cream	крем (ч) проти зморшок	[krɛm ˈprɔtɨ ˈzmɔrʃok]
day (as adj)	денний	[ˈdɛnɨj]
night (as adj)	нічний	[nitʃˈnɨj]
tampon	тампон (ч)	[tamˈpɔn]
toilet paper (toilet roll)	туалетний папір (ч)	[tuaˈlɛtnɨj paˈpir]
hair dryer	фен (ч)	[fɛn]

40. Watches. Clocks

watch (wristwatch)	годинник (ч)	[ɦoˈdɨnɨk]
dial	циферблат (ч)	[tsɨfɛrbˈlat]
hand (clock, watch)	стрілка (ж)	[ˈstrilka]
metal bracelet	браслет (ч)	[brasˈlɛt]
watch strap	ремінець (ч)	[rɛmiˈnɛts]
battery	батарейка (ж)	[bataˈrɛjka]
to be flat (battery)	сісти	[ˈsistɨ]
to change a battery	поміняти батарейку	[pomiˈnʲatɨ bataˈrɛjku]
to run fast	поспішати	[pospiˈʃatɨ]
to run slow	відставати	[widstaˈwatɨ]
wall clock	годинник (ч)	[ɦoˈdɨnɨk]
hourglass	годинник (ч) пісковий	[ɦoˈdɨnɨk pisˈkɔwɨj]
sundial	годинник (ч) сонячний	[ɦoˈdɨnɨk ˈsɔnʲatʃnɨj]
alarm clock	будильник (ч)	[buˈdɨlʲnɨk]
watchmaker	годинникар (ч)	[ɦodɨnɨˈkar]
to repair (vt)	ремонтувати	[rɛmontuˈwatɨ]

EVERYDAY EXPERIENCE

41. Money

money	гроші (мн)	['ɦrɔʃi]
currency exchange	обмін (ч)	['ɔbmin]
exchange rate	курс (ч)	[kurs]
cashpoint	банкомат (ч)	[banko'mat]
coin	монета (ж)	[mo'nɛta]
dollar	долар (ч)	['dɔlar]
euro	євро (ч)	['ɛwro]
lira	ліра (ж)	['lira]
Deutschmark	марка (ж)	['marka]
franc	франк (ч)	['frank]
pound sterling	фунт (ч)	['funt]
yen	ієна (ж)	[i'ɛna]
debt	борг (ч)	['bɔrɦ]
debtor	боржник (ч)	[borʒ'nik]
to lend (money)	позичити	[po'ziʧiti]
to borrow (vi, vt)	взяти в борг	['wzʲati w borɦ]
bank	банк (ч)	[bank]
account	рахунок (ч)	[ra'hunok]
to deposit into the account	покласти на рахунок	[pok'lasti na ra'hunok]
to withdraw (vt)	зняти з рахунку	['znʲati z ra'hunku]
credit card	кредитна картка (ж)	[krɛ'ditna 'kartka]
cash	готівка (ж)	[ɦo'tiwka]
cheque	чек (ч)	[ʧɛk]
to write a cheque	виписати чек	['wipisati 'ʧɛk]
chequebook	чекова книжка (ж)	['ʧɛkowa 'kniʒka]
wallet	гаманець (ч)	[ɦama'nɛts]
purse	гаманець (ч)	[ɦama'nɛts]
safe	сейф (ч)	[sɛjf]
heir	спадкоємець (ч)	[spadko'ɛmɛts]
inheritance	спадщина (с)	['spadɕina]
fortune (wealth)	статок (ч)	['statok]
lease	оренда (ж)	[o'rɛnda]
rent (money)	квартирна плата (ж)	[kwar'tirna 'plata]
to rent (sth from sb)	наймати	[naj'mati]
price	ціна (ж)	[ʦi'na]
cost	вартість (ж)	['wartistʲ]
sum	сума (ж)	['suma]

to spend (vt)	витрачати	[witra'tʃati]
expenses	витрати (мн)	['witrati]
to economize (vi, vt)	економити	[ɛko'nɔmiti]
economical	економний	[ɛko'nɔmnij]

to pay (vi, vt)	платити	[pla'titi]
payment	оплата (ж)	[op'lata]
change (give the ~)	решта (ж)	['rɛʃta]

tax	податок (ч)	[po'datok]
fine	штраф (ч)	[ʃtraf]
to fine (vt)	штрафувати	[ʃtrafu'wati]

42. Post. Postal service

post office	пошта (ж)	['pɔʃta]
post (letters, etc.)	пошта (ж)	['pɔʃta]
postman	листоноша (ч)	[listo'nɔʃa]
opening hours	години (мн) роботи	[ɦo'dini ro'bɔti]

letter	лист (ч)	[list]
registered letter	рекомендований лист (ч)	[rɛkomɛn'dɔwanij list]
postcard	листівка (ж)	[lis'tiwka]
telegram	телеграма (ж)	[tɛlɛ'ɦrama]
parcel	посилка (ж)	[po'siɫka]
money transfer	грошовий переказ (ч)	[ɦroʃo'wij pɛ'rɛkaz]

to receive (vt)	отримати	[ot'rimati]
to send (vt)	відправити	[wid'prawiti]
sending	відправлення (с)	[wid'prawlɛnʲa]

address	адреса (ж)	[ad'rɛsa]
postcode	індекс (ч)	['indɛks]
sender	відправник (ч)	[wid'prawnik]
receiver	одержувач (ч)	[o'dɛrʒuwatʃ]

| name (first name) | ім'я (с) | [i'mʲʲa] |
| surname (last name) | прізвище (с) | ['prizwiçɛ] |

postage rate	тариф (ч)	[ta'rif]
standard (adj)	звичайний	[zwi'tʃajnij]
economical (adj)	економічний	[ɛkono'mitʃnij]

weight	вага (ж)	[wa'ɦa]
to weigh (~ letters)	важити	['waʒiti]
envelope	конверт (ч)	[kon'wɛrt]
postage stamp	марка (ж)	['marka]

43. Banking

| bank | банк (ч) | [bank] |
| branch (of a bank) | відділення (с) | [wid'dilɛnʲa] |

| consultant | консультант (ч) | [konsuɫˈtant] |
| manager (director) | управляючий (ч) | [uprawˈlʲaˈutʃij] |

bank account	рахунок (ч)	[raˈhunok]
account number	номер (ч) рахунка	[ˈnɔmɛr raˈhunka]
current account	поточний рахунок (ч)	[poˈtɔtʃnij raˈhunok]
deposit account	накопичувальний рахунок (ч)	[nakoˈpitʃuwalʲnij raˈhunok]

to open an account	відкрити рахунок	[widˈkriti raˈhunok]
to close the account	закрити рахунок	[zaˈkriti raˈhunok]
to deposit into the account	покласти на рахунок	[pokˈlasti na raˈhunok]
to withdraw (vt)	зняти з рахунку	[ˈznʲati z raˈhunku]

deposit	внесок (ч)	[ˈwnɛsok]
to make a deposit	зробити внесок	[zroˈbiti ˈwnɛsok]
wire transfer	переказ (ч)	[pɛˈrɛkaz]
to wire, to transfer	зробити переказ	[zroˈbiti pɛˈrɛkaz]

| sum | сума (ж) | [ˈsuma] |
| How much? | Скільки? | [ˈskilʲki] |

| signature | підпис (ч) | [ˈpidpis] |
| to sign (vt) | підписати | [pidpiˈsati] |

credit card	кредитна картка (ж)	[krɛˈditna ˈkartka]
code (PIN code)	код (ч)	[kod]
credit card number	номер (ч) кредитної картки	[ˈnɔmɛr krɛˈditnoji ˈkartki]
cashpoint	банкомат (ч)	[bankoˈmat]

cheque	чек (ч)	[tʃɛk]
to write a cheque	виписати чек	[ˈwipisati ˈtʃɛk]
chequebook	чекова книжка (ж)	[ˈtʃɛkowa ˈkniʒka]

loan (bank ~)	кредит (ч)	[krɛˈdit]
to apply for a loan	звертатися за кредитом	[zwɛrˈtatisʲa za krɛˈditom]
to get a loan	брати кредит	[ˈbrati krɛˈdit]
to give a loan	надавати кредит	[nadaˈwati krɛˈdit]
guarantee	застава (ж)	[zaˈstawa]

44. Telephone. Phone conversation

telephone	телефон (ч)	[tɛlɛˈfon]
mobile phone	мобільний телефон (ч)	[moˈbilʲnij tɛlɛˈfon]
answerphone	автовідповідач (ч)	[awtowidpowiˈdatʃ]

| to call (by phone) | телефонувати | [tɛlɛfonuˈwati] |
| call, ring | дзвінок (ч) | [dzwiˈnɔk] |

to dial a number	набрати номер	[nabˈrati ˈnɔmɛr]
Hello!	Алло!	[aˈlɔ]
to ask (vt)	запитати	[zapiˈtati]
to answer (vi, vt)	відповісти	[widpoˈwisti]
to hear (vt)	чути	[ˈtʃuti]

well (adv)	добре	['dɔbrɛ]
not well (adv)	погано	[po'ɦano]
noises (interference)	перешкоди (мн)	[pɛrɛʃ'kɔdi]

receiver	трубка (ж)	['trubka]
to pick up (~ the phone)	зняти трубку	['znʲati 'trubku]
to hang up (~ the phone)	покласти трубку	[pok'lasti t'rubku]

busy (engaged)	зайнятий	['zajnʲatij]
to ring (ab. phone)	дзвонити	[dzwo'niti]
telephone book	телефонна книга (ж)	[tɛlɛ'fona 'kniɦa]

local (adj)	місцевий	[mis'tsɛwij]
local call	місцевий зв'язок (ч)	[mis'tsɛwij 'zwʲazok]
trunk (e.g. ~ call)	міжміський	[miʒmisʲ'kij]
trunk call	міжміський зв'язок (ч)	[miʒmisʲ'kij 'zwʲazok]
international (adj)	міжнародний	[miʒna'rɔdnij]
international call	міжнародний зв'язок (ч)	[miʒna'rɔdnij 'zwʲazok]

45. Mobile telephone

mobile phone	мобільний телефон (ч)	[mo'bilʲnij tɛlɛ'fɔn]
display	дисплей (ч)	[dis'plɛj]
button	кнопка (ж)	['knɔpka]
SIM card	SIM-карта (ж)	[sim 'karta]

battery	батарея (ж)	[bata'rɛʲa]
to be flat (battery)	розрядитися	[rozrʲa'ditisʲa]
charger	зарядний пристрій (ч)	[za'rʲadnij 'pristrij]

menu	меню (с)	[mɛ'nʲu]
settings	настройки (мн)	[na'strɔjki]
tune (melody)	мелодія (ж)	[mɛ'lɔdiʲa]
to select (vt)	вибрати	['wibrati]

calculator	калькулятор (ч)	[kalʲku'lʲator]
voice mail	автовідповідач (ч)	[awtowidpowi'datʃ]
alarm clock	будильник (ч)	[bu'dilʲnik]
contacts	телефонна книга (ж)	[tɛlɛ'fona 'kniɦa]

| SMS (text message) | SMS-повідомлення (с) | [ɛsɛ'mɛs powi'dɔmlɛnʲa] |
| subscriber | абонент (ч) | [abo'nɛnt] |

46. Stationery

| ballpoint pen | авторучка (ж) | [awto'rutʃka] |
| fountain pen | ручка-перо (с) | ['rutʃka pɛ'rɔ] |

pencil	олівець (ч)	[oli'wɛts]
highlighter	маркер (ч)	['markɛr]
felt-tip pen	фломастер (ч)	[flo'mastɛr]
notepad	блокнот (ч)	[blok'nɔt]

diary	щоденник (ч)	[ɕo'dɛnik]
ruler	лінійка (ж)	[li'nijka]
calculator	калькулятор (ч)	[kalʲku'lʲator]
rubber	гумка (ж)	['ɦumka]
drawing pin	кнопка (ж)	['knɔpka]
paper clip	скріпка (ж)	['skripka]

glue	клей (ч)	[klɛj]
stapler	степлер (ч)	['stɛplɛr]
hole punch	діркопробивач (ч)	[dirkoprobi'watʃ]
pencil sharpener	стругачка (ж)	[stru'ɦatʃka]

47. Foreign languages

language	мова (ж)	['mɔwa]
foreign language	іноземна мова (ж)	[ino'zɛmna 'mɔwa]
to study (vt)	вивчати	[wiw'tʃati]
to learn (language, etc.)	вчити	['wtʃiti]

to read (vi, vt)	читати	[tʃi'tati]
to speak (vi, vt)	розмовляти	[rozmow'lʲati]
to understand (vt)	розуміти	[rozu'miti]
to write (vt)	писати	[pi'sati]

fast (adv)	швидко	['ʃwidko]
slowly (adv)	повільно	[po'wilʲno]
fluently (adv)	вільно	['wilʲno]

rules	правила (мн)	['prawila]
grammar	граматика (ж)	[ɦra'matika]
vocabulary	лексика (ж)	['lɛksika]
phonetics	фонетика (ж)	[fo'nɛtika]

textbook	підручник (ч)	[pid'rutʃnik]
dictionary	словник (ч)	[slow'nik]
teach-yourself book	самовчитель (ч)	[samow'tʃitɛlʲ]
phrasebook	розмовник (ч)	[roz'mɔwnik]

cassette, tape	касета (ж)	[ka'sɛta]
videotape	відеокасета (ж)	['widɛo ka'sɛta]
CD, compact disc	CD-диск (ч)	[si'di disk]
DVD	DVD (ч)	[diwi'di]

alphabet	алфавіт (ч)	[alfa'wit]
to spell (vt)	говорити по буквах	[ɦowo'riti po 'bukwah]
pronunciation	вимова (ж)	[wi'mɔwa]

accent	акцент (ч)	[ak'tsɛnt]
with an accent	з акцентом	[z ak'tsɛntom]
without an accent	без акценту (ч)	[bɛz ak'tsɛntu]

word	слово (с)	['slɔwo]
meaning	сенс (ч)	[sɛns]
course (e.g. a French ~)	курси (мн)	['kursi]

| to sign up | записатися | [zapi'satisʲa] |
| teacher | викладач (ч) | [wɨkla'datʃ] |

translation (process)	переклад (ч)	[pɛ'rɛklad]
translation (text, etc.)	переклад (ч)	[pɛ'rɛklad]
translator	перекладач (ч)	[pɛrɛkla'datʃ]
interpreter	перекладач (ч)	[pɛrɛkla'datʃ]

| polyglot | поліглот (ч) | [poliɦ'lɔt] |
| memory | пам'ять (ж) | ['pamʲatʲ] |

MEALS. RESTAURANT

48. Table setting

spoon	ложка (ж)	['lɔʒka]
knife	ніж (ч)	[niʒ]
fork	виделка (ж)	[wi'dɛlka]

cup (e.g., coffee ~)	чашка (ж)	['ʧaʃka]
plate (dinner ~)	тарілка (ж)	[ta'rilka]
saucer	блюдце (с)	['blʲudtsɛ]
serviette	серветка (ж)	[sɛr'wɛtka]
toothpick	зубочистка (ж)	[zubo'ʧistka]

49. Restaurant

restaurant	ресторан (ч)	[rɛsto'ran]
coffee bar	кав'ярня (ж)	[ka'wʲarnʲa]
pub, bar	бар (ч)	[bar]
tearoom	чайна (ж)	['ʧajna]

waiter	офіціант (ч)	[ofitsi'ant]
waitress	офіціантка (ж)	[ofitsi'antka]
barman	бармен (ч)	[bar'mɛn]

menu	меню (с)	[mɛ'nʲu]
wine list	карта (ж) вин	['karta win]
to book a table	забронювати столик	[zabronʲu'wati 'stolik]

course, dish	страва (ж)	['strawa]
to order (meal)	замовити	[za'mowiti]
to make an order	зробити замовлення	[zro'biti za'mowlɛnʲa]

aperitif	аперитив (ч)	[apɛri'tiw]
starter	закуска (ж)	[za'kuska]
dessert, pudding	десерт (ч)	[dɛ'sɛrt]

bill	рахунок (ч)	[ra'hunok]
to pay the bill	оплатити рахунок	[opla'titi ra'hunok]
to give change	дати решту	['dati 'rɛʃtu]
tip	чайові (мн)	[ʧaʲo'wi]

50. Meals

food	їжа (ж)	['jiʒa]
to eat (vi, vt)	їсти	['jisti]

breakfast	снiданок (ч)	[sni'danok]
to have breakfast	снiдати	['snidati]
lunch	обiд (ч)	[o'bid]
to have lunch	обiдати	[o'bidati]
dinner	вечеря (ж)	[wɛ'tʃɛrʲa]
to have dinner	вечеряти	[wɛ'tʃɛrʲati]

| appetite | апетит (ч) | [apɛ'tit] |
| Enjoy your meal! | Смачного! | [smatʃ'noɦo] |

to open (~ a bottle)	вiдкривати	[widkri'wati]
to spill (liquid)	пролити	[pro'liti]
to spill out (vi)	пролитись	[pro'litisʲ]

to boil (vi)	кипiти	[ki'piti]
to boil (vt)	кип'ятити	[kipʲa'titi]
boiled (~ water)	кип'ячений	[kipʲa'tʃɛnij]
to chill, cool down (vt)	охолодити	[oholo'diti]
to chill (vi)	охолоджуватись	[oho'lɔdʒuwatisʲ]

| taste, flavour | смак (ч) | [smak] |
| aftertaste | присмак (ч) | ['prismak] |

to slim down (lose weight)	худнути	['hudnuti]
diet	дiєта (ж)	[di'ɛta]
vitamin	вiтамiн (ч)	[wita'min]
calorie	калорiя (ж)	[ka'lɔrʲa]
vegetarian (n)	вегетарiанець (ч)	[wɛɦɛtari'anɛts]
vegetarian (adj)	вегетарiанський	[wɛɦɛtari'ansʲkij]

fats (nutrient)	жири (мн)	[ʒi'ri]
proteins	бiлки (мн)	[bil'ki]
carbohydrates	вуглеводи (ч)	[wuɦlɛ'wɔdi]
slice (of lemon, ham)	скибка (ж)	['skibka]
piece (of cake, pie)	шматок (ч)	[ʃma'tɔk]
crumb (of bread, cake, etc.)	крихта (ж)	['krihta]

51. Cooked dishes

course, dish	страва (ж)	['strawa]
cuisine	кухня (ж)	['kuhnʲa]
recipe	рецепт (ч)	[rɛ'tsɛpt]
portion	порцiя (ж)	['portsiʲa]

| salad | салат (ч) | [sa'lat] |
| soup | юшка (ж) | ['ʲuʃka] |

clear soup (broth)	бульйон (ч)	[bul'ɔn]
sandwich (bread)	канапка (ж)	[ka'napka]
fried eggs	яєчня (ж)	[ja'ɛʃnʲa]

hamburger (beefburger)	гамбургер (ч)	['ɦamburɦɛr]
beefsteak	бiфштекс (ч)	[bif'ʃtɛks]
side dish	гарнiр (ч)	[ɦar'nir]

spaghetti	спагеті (мн)	[spa'hɛti]
mash	картопляне пюре (c)	[kartop'lʲanɛ pʲu'rɛ]
pizza	піца (ж)	['piʦa]
porridge (oatmeal, etc.)	каша (ж)	['kaʃa]
omelette	омлет (ч)	[om'lɛt]

boiled (e.g. ~ beef)	варений	[wa'rɛnij]
smoked (adj)	копчений	[kop'ʧɛnij]
fried (adj)	смажений	['smaʒɛnij]
dried (adj)	сушений	['suʃɛnij]
frozen (adj)	заморожений	[zamo'roʒɛnij]
pickled (adj)	маринований	[mari'nɔwanij]

sweet (sugary)	солодкий	[so'lɔdkij]
salty (adj)	солоний	[so'lɔnij]
cold (adj)	холодний	[ho'lɔdnij]
hot (adj)	гарячий	[ha'rʲaʧij]
bitter (adj)	гіркий	[hir'kij]
tasty (adj)	смачний	[smaʧ'nij]

to cook in boiling water	варити	[wa'riti]
to cook (dinner)	готувати	[hotu'wati]
to fry (vt)	смажити	['smaʒiti]
to heat up (food)	розігрівати	[rozihri'wati]

to salt (vt)	солити	[so'liti]
to pepper (vt)	перчити	[pɛr'ʧiti]
to grate (vt)	терти	['tɛrti]
peel (n)	шкірка (ж)	['ʃkirka]
to peel (vt)	чистити	['ʧistiti]

52. Food

meat	м'ясо (c)	['mʲʲaso]
chicken	курка (ж)	['kurka]
poussin	курча (c)	[kur'ʧa]
duck	качка (ж)	['kaʧka]
goose	гусак (ч)	[hu'sak]
game	дичина (ж)	[diʧi'na]
turkey	індичка (ж)	[in'diʧka]

pork	свинина (ж)	[swi'nina]
veal	телятина (ж)	[tɛ'lʲatina]
lamb	баранина (ж)	[ba'ranina]
beef	яловичина (ж)	['ʲalowiʧina]
rabbit	кріль (ч)	[krilʲ]

sausage (bologna, etc.)	ковбаса (ж)	[kowba'sa]
vienna sausage (frankfurter)	сосиска (ж)	[so'siska]
bacon	бекон (ч)	[bɛ'kɔn]
ham	шинка (ж)	['ʃinka]
gammon	окіст (ч)	['ɔkist]
pâté	паштет (ч)	[paʃ'tɛt]
liver	печінка (ж)	[pɛ'ʧinka]

mince (minced meat)	фарш (ч)	[farʃ]
tongue	язик (ч)	[ja'zik]
egg	яйце (с)	[jaj'tsɛ]
eggs	яйця (мн)	[ˈjajtsʲa]
egg white	білок (ч)	[bi'lɔk]
egg yolk	жовток (ч)	[ʒow'tɔk]
fish	риба (ж)	['riba]
seafood	морепродукти (мн)	[morɛpro'dukti]
caviar	ікра (ж)	[ik'ra]
crab	краб (ч)	[krab]
prawn	креветка (ж)	[krɛ'wɛtka]
oyster	устриця (ж)	['ustritsʲa]
spiny lobster	лангуст (ч)	[lan'ɦust]
octopus	восьминіг (ч)	[wosʲmiˈniɦ]
squid	кальмар (ч)	[kalʲ'mar]
sturgeon	осетрина (ж)	[osɛt'rina]
salmon	лосось (ч)	[lo'sɔsʲ]
halibut	палтус (ч)	['paltus]
cod	тріска (ж)	[tris'ka]
mackerel	скумбрія (ж)	['skumbriʲa]
tuna	тунець (ч)	[tu'nɛts]
eel	вугор (ч)	[wu'ɦor]
trout	форель (ж)	[fo'rɛlʲ]
sardine	сардина (ж)	[sar'dina]
pike	щука (ж)	['ɕuka]
herring	оселедець (ч)	[osɛ'lɛdɛts]
bread	хліб (ч)	[hlib]
cheese	сир (ч)	[sir]
sugar	цукор (ч)	['tsukor]
salt	сіль (ж)	[silʲ]
rice	рис (ч)	[ris]
pasta (macaroni)	макарони (мн)	[maka'rɔni]
noodles	локшина (ж)	[lokʃi'na]
butter	вершкове масло (с)	[wɛrʃ'kɔwɛ 'maslo]
vegetable oil	олія (ж) рослинна	[o'liʲa ros'lina]
sunflower oil	соняшникова олія (ж)	['sɔnʲaʃnikowa o'liʲa]
margarine	маргарин (ч)	[marɦa'rin]
olives	оливки (мн)	[o'liwki]
olive oil	олія (ж) оливкова	[o'liʲa o'liwkowa]
milk	молоко (с)	[molo'kɔ]
condensed milk	згущене молоко (с)	['zɦuɕɛnɛ molo'kɔ]
yogurt	йогурт (ч)	['jɔɦurt]
soured cream	сметана (ж)	[smɛ'tana]
cream (of milk)	вершки (мн)	[wɛrʃ'ki]
mayonnaise	майонез (ч)	[maʲo'nɛz]

buttercream	крем (ч)	[krɛm]
groats (barley ~, etc.)	крупа (ж)	[kru'pa]
flour	борошно (с)	['bɔrɔʃnɔ]
tinned food	консерви (мн)	[kon'sɛrwɨ]

cornflakes	кукурудзяні пластівці (мн)	[kuku'rudzʲani plastiw'tsi]
honey	мед (ч)	[mɛdʒ]
jam	джем (ч)	[dʒɛm]
chewing gum	жувальна гумка (ж)	[ʒu'walʲna 'ɦumka]

53. Drinks

water	вода (ж)	[wo'da]
drinking water	питна вода (ж)	[pɨt'na wo'da]
mineral water	мінеральна вода (ж)	[minɛ'ralʲna wo'da]

still (adj)	без газу	[bɛz 'ɦazu]
carbonated (adj)	газований	[ɦa'zɔwanɨj]
sparkling (adj)	з газом	[z 'ɦazom]
ice	лід (ч)	[lid]
with ice	з льодом	[z lʲodom]

non-alcoholic (adj)	безалкогольний	[bɛzalko'ɦɔlʲnɨj]
soft drink	безалкогольний напій (ч)	[bɛzalko'ɦɔlʲnij na'pij]
refreshing drink	прохолодній напій (ч)	[proho'lɔdnij na'pij]
lemonade	лимонад (ч)	[lɨmo'nad]

spirits	алкогольні напої (мн)	[alko'ɦɔlʲni na'pojі]
wine	вино (с)	[wɨ'nɔ]
white wine	біле вино (с)	['bilɛ wɨ'nɔ]
red wine	червоне вино (с)	[tʃɛr'wɔnɛ wɨ'nɔ]

liqueur	лікер (ч)	[li'kɛr]
champagne	шампанське (с)	[ʃam'pansʲkɛ]
vermouth	вермут (ч)	['wɛrmut]

whisky	віскі (с)	['wiski]
vodka	горілка (ж)	[ɦo'rilka]
gin	джин (ч)	[dʒin]
cognac	коньяк (ч)	[ko'nʲak]
rum	ром (ч)	[rom]

coffee	кава (ж)	['kawa]
black coffee	чорна кава (ж)	['tʃɔrna 'kawa]
white coffee	кава (ж) з молоком	['kawa z molo'kɔm]
cappuccino	кава (ж) з вершками	['kawa z wɛrʃ'kamɨ]
instant coffee	розчинна кава (ж)	[roz'tʃɨna 'kawa]

milk	молоко (с)	[molo'kɔ]
cocktail	коктейль (ч)	[kok'tɛjlʲ]
milkshake	молочний коктейль (ч)	[mo'lɔtʃnɨj kok'tɛjlʲ]

| juice | сік (ч) | [sik] |
| tomato juice | томатний сік (ч) | [to'matnɨj 'sik] |

| orange juice | апельсиновий сік (ч) | [apɛlʲ'sinowij sik] |
| freshly squeezed juice | свіжовижатий сік (ч) | [swiʒo'wiʒatij sik] |

beer	пиво (с)	['piwo]
lager	світле пиво (с)	['switlɛ 'piwo]
bitter	темне пиво (с)	['tɛmnɛ 'piwo]

tea	чай (ч)	[ʧaj]
black tea	чорний чай (ч)	['ʧornij ʧaj]
green tea	зелений чай (ч)	[zɛ'lɛnij ʧaj]

54. Vegetables

| vegetables | овочі (мн) | ['owoʧi] |
| greens | зелень (ж) | ['zɛlɛnʲ] |

tomato	помідор (ч)	[pomi'dɔr]
cucumber	огірок (ч)	[ohi'rɔk]
carrot	морква (ж)	['mɔrkwa]
potato	картопля (ж)	[kar'toplʲa]
onion	цибуля (ж)	[ʦi'bulʲa]
garlic	часник (ч)	[ʧas'nik]

cabbage	капуста (ж)	[ka'pusta]
cauliflower	кольорова капуста (ж)	[kolʲo'rowa ka'pusta]
Brussels sprouts	брюссельська капуста (ж)	[brʲu'sɛlʲsʲka ka'pusta]
broccoli	капуста броколі (ж)	[ka'pusta 'brɔkoli]
beetroot	буряк (ч)	[bu'rʲak]
aubergine	баклажан (ч)	[bakla'ʒan]
courgette	кабачок (ч)	[kaba'ʧɔk]
pumpkin	гарбуз (ч)	[har'buz]
turnip	ріпа (ж)	['ripa]

parsley	петрушка (ж)	[pɛt'ruʃka]
dill	кріп (ч)	[krip]
lettuce	салат (ч)	[sa'lat]
celery	селера (ж)	[sɛ'lɛra]
asparagus	спаржа (ж)	['sparʒa]
spinach	шпинат (ч)	[ʃpi'nat]
pea	горох (ч)	[ho'rɔh]
beans	боби (мн)	[bo'bi]
maize	кукурудза (ж)	[kuku'rudza]
kidney bean	квасоля (ж)	[kwa'solʲa]

sweet paper	перець (ч)	['pɛrɛʦ]
radish	редька (ж)	['rɛdʲka]
artichoke	артишок (ч)	[artiʲʃɔk]

55. Fruits. Nuts

| fruit | фрукт (ч) | [frukt] |
| apple | яблуко (с) | [ʲabluko] |

pear	груша (ж)	['ɦruʃa]
lemon	лимон (ч)	[liˈmɔn]
orange	апельсин (ч)	[apɛlʲˈsin]
strawberry (garden ~)	полуниця (ж)	[poluˈnitsʲa]
tangerine	мандарин (ч)	[mandaˈrin]
plum	слива (ж)	['sliwa]
peach	персик (ч)	['pɛrsik]
apricot	абрикос (ч)	[abriˈkɔs]
raspberry	малина (ж)	[maˈlina]
pineapple	ананас (ч)	[anaˈnas]
banana	банан (ч)	[baˈnan]
watermelon	кавун (ч)	[kaˈwun]
grape	виноград (ч)	[winoˈɦrad]
sour cherry	вишня (ж)	['wiʃnʲa]
sweet cherry	черешня (ж)	[ʧɛˈrɛʃnʲa]
melon	диня (ж)	['dinʲa]
grapefruit	грейпфрут (ч)	[ɦrɛjpˈfrut]
avocado	авокадо (с)	[awoˈkado]
papaya	папайя (ж)	[paˈpaʲa]
mango	манго (с)	['manɦo]
pomegranate	гранат (ч)	[ɦraˈnat]
redcurrant	порічки (мн)	[poˈriʧki]
blackcurrant	чорна смородина (ж)	['ʧɔrna smoˈrɔdina]
gooseberry	аґрус (ч)	['agrus]
bilberry	чорниця (ж)	[ʧorˈnitsʲa]
blackberry	ожина (ж)	[oˈʒina]
raisin	родзинки (мн)	[roˈdzinki]
fig	інжир (ч)	[inˈʒir]
date	фінік (ч)	['finik]
peanut	арахіс (ч)	[aˈrahis]
almond	мигдаль (ч)	[miɦˈdalʲ]
walnut	горіх (ч) волоський	[ɦoˈrih woˈlɔsʲkij]
hazelnut	ліщина (ж)	[liˈɕina]
coconut	горіх (ч) кокосовий	[ɦoˈrih koˈkɔsowij]
pistachios	фісташки (мн)	[fisˈtaʃki]

56. Bread. Sweets

bakers' confectionery (pastry)	кондитерські вироби (мн)	[konˈditɛrsʲki ˈwirobi]
bread	хліб (ч)	[hlib]
biscuits	печиво (с)	['pɛʧiwo]
chocolate (n)	шоколад (ч)	[ʃokoˈlad]
chocolate (as adj)	шоколадний	[ʃokoˈladnij]
candy (wrapped)	цукерка (ж)	[tsuˈkɛrka]
cake (e.g. cupcake)	тістечко (с)	['tistɛʧko]
cake (e.g. birthday ~)	торт (ч)	[tort]
pie (e.g. apple ~)	пиріг (ч)	[piˈriɦ]

filling (for cake, pie)	начинка (ж)	[na'ʧinka]
jam (whole fruit jam)	варення (с)	[wa'rɛnʲa]
marmalade	мармелад (ч)	[marmɛ'lad]
wafers	вафлі (мн)	['wafli]
ice-cream	морозиво (с)	[mo'rɔziwo]

57. Spices

salt	сіль (ж)	[silʲ]
salty (adj)	солоний	[so'lɔnij]
to salt (vt)	солити	[so'liti]

black pepper	чорний перець (ч)	['ʧɔrnij 'pɛrɛts]
red pepper (milled ~)	червоний перець (ч)	[ʧɛr'wɔnij 'pɛrɛts]
mustard	гірчиця (ж)	[hir'ʧitsʲa]
horseradish	хрін (ч)	[hrin]

condiment	приправа (ж)	[prip'rawa]
spice	прянощі (мн)	[prʲa'nɔɕi]
sauce	соус (ч)	['sɔus]
vinegar	оцет (ч)	['ɔtsɛt]

anise	аніс (ч)	['anis]
basil	базилік (ч)	[bazi'lik]
cloves	гвоздика (ж)	[ɦwoz'dika]
ginger	імбир (ч)	[im'bir]
coriander	коріандр (ч)	[kori'andr]
cinnamon	кориця (ж)	[ko'ritsʲa]

sesame	кунжут (ч)	[kun'ʒut]
bay leaf	лавровий лист (ч)	[law'rɔwij list]
paprika	паприка (ж)	['paprika]
caraway	кмин (ч)	[kmin]
saffron	шафран (ч)	[ʃaf'ran]

PERSONAL INFORMATION. FAMILY

58. Personal information. Forms

name (first name)	ім'я (с)	[i'mʲa]
surname (last name)	прізвище (с)	['prizwiꞔɛ]
date of birth	дата (ж) народження	['data na'rɔdʒɛnʲa]
place of birth	місце (с) народження	['misꞔɛ na'rɔdʒɛnʲa]
nationality	національність (ж)	[naꞔio'nalʲnistʲ]
place of residence	місце (с) проживання	['misꞔɛ prɔʒiʲ'wanʲa]
country	країна (ж)	[kra'ji̇na]
profession (occupation)	професія (ж)	[pro'fɛsiʲa]
gender, sex	стать (ж)	[statʲ]
height	зріст (ч)	[zrist]
weight	вага (ж)	[wa'ɦa]

59. Family members. Relatives

mother	мати (ж)	['mati]
father	батько (ч)	['batʲko]
son	син (ч)	[sin]
daughter	дочка (ж)	[dotʲʲka]
younger daughter	молодша дочка (ж)	[mo'lɔdʃa dotʲʲka]
younger son	молодший син (ч)	[mo'lɔdʃij sin]
eldest daughter	старша дочка (ж)	['starʃa dotʲʲka]
eldest son	старший син (ч)	['starʃij sin]
brother	брат (ч)	[brat]
sister	сестра (ж)	[sɛst'ra]
cousin (masc.)	двоюрідний брат (ч)	[dwoʲu'ridnij brat]
cousin (fem.)	двоюрідна сестра (ж)	[dwoʲu'ridna sɛst'ra]
mummy	мати (ж)	['mati]
dad, daddy	тато (ч)	['tato]
parents	батьки (мн)	[batʲ'ki]
child	дитина (ж)	[di'tina]
children	діти (мн)	['diti]
grandmother	бабуся (ж)	[ba'busʲa]
grandfather	дід (ч)	['did]
grandson	онук (ч)	[o'nuk]
granddaughter	онука (ж)	[o'nuka]
grandchildren	онуки (мн)	[o'nuki]
uncle	дядько (ч)	['dʲadʲko]
aunt	тітка (ж)	['titka]

| nephew | племінник (ч) | [plɛ'minik] |
| niece | племінниця (ж) | [plɛ'minitsʲa] |

mother-in-law (wife's mother)	теща (ж)	['tɛɕa]
father-in-law (husband's father)	свекор (ч)	['swɛkor]
son-in-law (daughter's husband)	зять (ч)	[zʲatʲ]
stepmother	мачуха (ж)	['matʃuha]
stepfather	вітчим (ч)	['witʃim]

infant	немовля (с)	[nɛmow'lʲa]
baby (infant)	немовля (с)	[nɛmow'lʲa]
little boy, kid	малюк (ч)	[ma'lʲuk]

wife	дружина (ж)	[dru'ʒina]
husband	чоловік (ч)	[tʃolo'wik]
spouse (husband)	чоловік (ч)	[tʃolo'wik]
spouse (wife)	дружина (ж)	[dru'ʒina]

married (masc.)	одружений	[od'ruʒɛnij]
married (fem.)	заміжня	[za'miʒnʲa]
single (unmarried)	холостий	[holos'tij]
bachelor	холостяк (ч)	[holos'tʲak]
divorced (masc.)	розведений	[roz'wɛdɛnij]
widow	вдова (ж)	[wdo'wa]
widower	вдівець (ч)	[wdi'wɛts]

relative	родич (ч)	['rɔditʃ]
close relative	близький родич (ч)	[blizʲ'kij 'rɔditʃ]
distant relative	далекий родич (ч)	[da'lɛkij 'rɔditʃ]
relatives	рідні (мн)	['ridni]

orphan (boy or girl)	сирота (ч)	[siro'ta]
guardian (of a minor)	опікун (ч)	[opi'kun]
to adopt (a boy)	усиновити	[usino'witi]
to adopt (a girl)	удочерити	[udotʃɛ'riti]

60. Friends. Colleagues

friend (masc.)	товариш (ч)	[to'wariʃ]
friend (fem.)	подруга (ж)	['podruɦa]
friendship	дружба (ж)	['druʒba]
to be friends	дружити	[dru'ʒiti]

pal (masc.)	приятель (ч)	['prijatɛlʲ]
pal (fem.)	приятелька (ж)	['prijatɛlʲka]
partner	партнер (ч)	[part'nɛr]

chief (boss)	шеф (ч)	[ʃɛf]
superior (n)	начальник (ч)	[na'tʃalʲnik]
subordinate (n)	підлеглий (ч)	[pid'lɛɦlij]
colleague	колега (ч)	[ko'lɛɦa]

acquaintance (person)	знайомий (ч)	[zna'jomij]
fellow traveller	попутник (ч)	[po'putnik]
classmate	однокласник (ч)	[odno'klasnik]

neighbour (masc.)	сусід (ч)	[su'sid]
neighbour (fem.)	сусідка (ж)	[su'sidka]
neighbours	сусіди (мн)	[su'sidi]

HUMAN BODY. MEDICINE

61. Head

head	голова (ж)	[ɦolo'wa]
face	обличчя (с)	[ob'litʃʲa]
nose	ніс (ч)	[nis]
mouth	рот (ч)	[rot]
eye	око (с)	['ɔko]
eyes	очі (мн)	['ɔtʃi]
pupil	зіниця (ч)	[zi'nitsʲa]
eyebrow	брова (ж)	[bro'wa]
eyelash	вія (ж)	['wiʲa]
eyelid	повіка (ж)	[po'wika]
tongue	язик (ч)	[ja'zik]
tooth	зуб (ч)	[zub]
lips	губи (мн)	['ɦubi]
cheekbones	вилиці (мн)	['wilitsi]
gum	ясна (мн)	['ʲasna]
palate	піднебіння (с)	[pidnɛ'binʲa]
nostrils	ніздрі (мн)	['nizdri]
chin	підборіддя (с)	[pidbo'riddʲa]
jaw	щелепа (ж)	[ɕɛ'lɛpa]
cheek	щока (ж)	[ɕo'ka]
forehead	чоло (с)	[tʃo'lɔ]
temple	скроня (ж)	['skrɔnʲa]
ear	вухо (с)	['wuɦo]
back of the head	потилиця (ж)	[po'tilitsʲa]
neck	шия (ж)	['ʃiʲa]
throat	горло (с)	['ɦɔrlo]
hair	волосся (с)	[wo'lɔssʲa]
hairstyle	зачіска (ж)	['zatʃiska]
haircut	стрижка (ж)	['striʒka]
wig	парик (ч)	[pa'rik]
moustache	вуса (мн)	['wusa]
beard	борода (ж)	[boro'da]
to have (a beard, etc.)	носити	[no'siti]
plait	коса (ж)	[ko'sa]
sideboards	бакенбарди (мн)	[bakɛn'bardi]
red-haired (adj)	рудий	[ru'dij]
grey (hair)	сивий	['siwij]
bald (adj)	лисий	['lisij]
bald patch	лисина (ж)	['lisina]

| ponytail | хвіст (ч) | [hwist] |
| fringe | чубчик (ч) | ['tʃubtʃik] |

62. Human body

| hand | кисть (ж) | [kistʲ] |
| arm | рука (ж) | [ru'ka] |

finger	палець (ч)	['palɛts]
thumb	великий палець (ч)	[wɛ'likij 'palɛts]
little finger	мізинець (ч)	[mi'zinɛts]
nail	ніготь (ч)	['nihotʲ]

fist	кулак (ч)	[ku'lak]
palm	долоня (ж)	[do'lonʲa]
wrist	зап'ясток (ч)	[za'pʲastok]
forearm	передпліччя (с)	[pɛrɛdp'litʃʲa]
elbow	лікоть (ч)	['likotʲ]
shoulder	плече (с)	[plɛ'tʃɛ]

leg	гомілка (ж)	[ho'milka]
foot	ступня (ж)	[stup'nʲa]
knee	коліно (с)	[ko'lino]
calf	литка (ж)	['litka]
hip	стегно (с)	[stɛh'nɔ]
heel	п'ятка (ж)	['pʲatka]

body	тіло (с)	['tilo]
stomach	живіт (ч)	[ʒi'wit]
chest	груди (мн)	['hrudi]
breast	груди (мн)	['hrudi]
flank	бік (ч)	[bik]
back	спина (ж)	['spina]
lower back	поперек (ч)	[popɛ'rɛk]
waist	талія (ж)	['taliʲa]

navel (belly button)	пупок (ч)	[pu'pɔk]
buttocks	сідниці (мн)	[sid'nitsi]
bottom	зад (ч)	[zad]

beauty spot	родимка (ж)	['rɔdimka]
birthmark (café au lait spot)	родима пляма (ж)	[ro'dima 'plʲama]
tattoo	татуювання (с)	[tatuʲu'wanʲa]
scar	рубець (ч)	[ru'bɛts]

63. Diseases

illness	хвороба (ж)	[hwo'rɔba]
to be ill	хворіти	[hwo'riti]
health	здоров'я (с)	[zdo'rɔwʲʲa]
runny nose (coryza)	нежить (ч)	['nɛʒitʲ]
tonsillitis	ангіна (ж)	[an'hina]

| cold (illness) | застуда (ж) | [za'studa] |
| to catch a cold | застудитися | [zastu'ditisʲa] |

bronchitis	бронхіт (ч)	[bron'hit]
pneumonia	запалення (с) легенів	[za'palɛnja lɛ'hɛniw]
flu, influenza	грип (ч)	[hrip]

shortsighted (adj)	короткозорий	[korotko'zɔrij]
longsighted (adj)	далекозорий	[dalɛko'zɔrij]
strabismus (crossed eyes)	косоокість (ж)	[koso'ɔkistʲ]
squint-eyed (adj)	косоокий	[koso'ɔkij]
cataract	катаракта (ж)	[kata'rakta]
glaucoma	глаукома (ж)	[hlau'kɔma]

stroke	інсульт (ч)	[in'sulʲt]
heart attack	інфаркт (ч)	[in'farkt]
myocardial infarction	інфаркт (ч) міокарду	[in'farkt mio'kardu]
paralysis	параліч (ч)	[para'litʃ]
to paralyse (vt)	паралізувати	[paralizu'wati]

allergy	алергія (ж)	[alɛr'hiʲa]
asthma	астма (ж)	['astma]
diabetes	діабет (ч)	[dia'bɛt]

| toothache | зубний біль (ч) | [zub'nij bilʲ] |
| caries | карієс (ч) | ['kariɛs] |

diarrhoea	діарея (ж)	[dia'rɛʲa]
constipation	запор (ч)	[za'pɔr]
stomach upset	розлад (ч) шлунку	['rɔzlad 'ʃlunku]
food poisoning	отруєння (с)	[ot'ruɛnʲa]
to get food poisoning	отруїтись	[otru'jitisʲ]

arthritis	артрит (ч)	[art'rit]
rickets	рахіт (ч)	[ra'hit]
rheumatism	ревматизм (ч)	[rɛwma'tizm]
atherosclerosis	атеросклероз (ч)	[atɛrosklɛ'rɔz]

gastritis	гастрит (ч)	[hast'rit]
appendicitis	апендицит (ч)	[apɛndi'tsit]
cholecystitis	холецистит (ч)	[holɛtsis'tit]
ulcer	виразка (ж)	['wirazka]

measles	кір (ч)	[kir]
rubella (German measles)	краснуха (ж)	[kras'nuha]
jaundice	жовтуха (ж)	[ʒow'tuha]
hepatitis	гепатит (ч)	[hɛpa'tit]

schizophrenia	шизофренія (ж)	[ʃizofrɛ'niʲa]
rabies (hydrophobia)	сказ (ч)	[skaz]
neurosis	невроз (ч)	[nɛw'rɔz]
concussion	струс (ч) мозку	['strus 'mɔzku]

cancer	рак (ч)	[rak]
sclerosis	склероз (ч)	[sklɛ'rɔz]
multiple sclerosis	розсіяний склероз (ч)	[roz'siʲanij sklɛ'rɔz]

alcoholism	алкоголізм (ч)	[alkoɦoˈlizm]
alcoholic (n)	алкоголік (ч)	[alkoˈɦolik]
syphilis	сифіліс (ч)	[ˈsifilis]
AIDS	СНІД (ч)	[snid]
tumour	пухлина (ж)	[puhˈlina]
malignant (adj)	злоякісна	[zloˈjakisna]
benign (adj)	доброякісний	[dobroˈjakisnij]
fever	гарячка (ж)	[ɦaˈrʲatʃka]
malaria	малярія (ж)	[malʲaˈrʲia]
gangrene	гангрена (ж)	[ɦanˈɦrɛna]
seasickness	морська хвороба (ж)	[morsʲˈka hwoˈrɔba]
epilepsy	епілепсія (ж)	[ɛpiˈlɛpsʲia]
epidemic	епідемія (ж)	[ɛpiˈdɛmʲia]
typhus	тиф (ч)	[tif]
tuberculosis	туберкульоз (ч)	[tubɛrkuˈlʲoz]
cholera	холера (ж)	[hoˈlɛra]
plague (bubonic ~)	чума (ж)	[ʧuˈma]

64. Symptoms. Treatments. Part 1

symptom	симптом (ч)	[simpˈtɔm]
temperature	температура (ж)	[tɛmpɛraˈtura]
high temperature (fever)	висока температура (ж)	[wiˈsɔka tɛmpɛraˈtura]
pulse (heartbeat)	пульс (ч)	[pulʲs]
dizziness (vertigo)	запаморочення (с)	[zaˈpamorotʃɛnʲia]
hot (adj)	гарячий	[ɦaˈrʲatʃij]
shivering	озноб (ч)	[ozˈnɔb]
pale (e.g. ~ face)	блідий	[bliˈdij]
cough	кашель (ч)	[ˈkaʃɛlʲ]
to cough (vi)	кашляти	[ˈkaʃlʲati]
to sneeze (vi)	чхати	[ˈʧhati]
faint	непритомність (ж)	[nɛpriˈtɔmnistʲ]
to faint (vi)	знепритомніти	[znɛpriˈtɔmniti]
bruise (hématome)	синець (ч)	[siˈnɛts]
bump (lump)	гуля (ж)	[ˈɦulʲa]
to bang (bump)	удaритись	[uˈdaritisʲ]
contusion (bruise)	забите місце (с)	[zaˈbitɛ ˈmistsɛ]
to get a bruise	забитися	[zaˈbitisʲa]
to limp (vi)	кульгати	[kulʲˈɦati]
dislocation	вивих (ч)	[ˈwiwih]
to dislocate (vt)	вивихнути	[ˈwiwihnuti]
fracture	перелом (ч)	[pɛrɛˈlɔm]
to have a fracture	дістати перелом	[disˈtati pɛrɛˈlɔm]
cut (e.g. paper ~)	поріз (ч)	[poˈriz]
to cut oneself	порізатися	[poˈrizatisʲa]
bleeding	кровотеча (ж)	[krowoˈtɛʧa]

burn (injury)	опік (ч)	['ɔpik]
to get burned	обпектися	[obpɛk'tisʲa]
to prick (vt)	уколоти	[uko'lɔti]
to prick oneself	уколотися	[uko'lɔtisʲa]
to injure (vt)	пошкодити	[poʃ'kɔditi]
injury	ушкодження (c)	[uʃ'kɔdʒɛnʲa]
wound	рана (ж)	['rana]
trauma	травма (ж)	['trawma]
to be delirious	марити	['mariti]
to stutter (vi)	заїкатися	[zaji'katisʲa]
sunstroke	сонячний удар (ч)	['sɔnʲatʃnij u'dar]

65. Symptoms. Treatments. Part 2

pain, ache	біль (ч)	[bilʲ]
splinter (in foot, etc.)	скалка (ж)	['skalka]
sweat (perspiration)	піт (ч)	[pit]
to sweat (perspire)	спітніти	[spit'niti]
vomiting	блювота (ж)	[blʲu'wɔta]
convulsions	судома (ж)	[su'dɔma]
pregnant (adj)	вагітна	[wa'ɦitna]
to be born	народитися	[naro'ditisʲa]
delivery, labour	пологи (мн)	[po'lɔɦi]
to deliver (~ a baby)	народжувати	[na'rɔdʒuwati]
abortion	аборт (ч)	[a'bɔrt]
breathing, respiration	дихання (c)	['diɦanʲa]
in-breath (inhalation)	вдих (ч)	[wdiɦ]
out-breath (exhalation)	видих (ч)	['widiɦ]
to exhale (breathe out)	видихнути	['widiɦnuti]
to inhale (vi)	зробити вдих	[zro'biti wdiɦ]
disabled person	інвалід (ч)	[inwa'lid]
cripple	каліка (ч)	[ka'lika]
drug addict	наркоман (ч)	[narko'man]
deaf (adj)	глухий (ч)	[ɦlu'ɦij]
mute (adj)	німий (ч)	[ni'mij]
deaf mute (adj)	глухонімий (ч)	[ɦluhoni'mij]
mad, insane (adj)	божевільний	[boʒɛ'wilʲnij]
madman (demented person)	божевільний (ч)	[boʒɛ'wilʲnij]
madwoman	божевільна (ж)	[boʒɛ'wilʲna]
to go insane	збожеволіти	[zboʒɛ'wɔliti]
gene	ген (ч)	[ɦɛn]
immunity	імунітет (ч)	[imuni'tɛt]
hereditary (adj)	спадковий	[spad'kɔwij]
congenital (adj)	вроджений	['wrɔdʒɛnij]

virus	вірус (ч)	['wirus]
microbe	мікроб (ч)	[mik'rɔb]
bacterium	бактерія (ж)	[bak'tɛriˈa]
infection	інфекція (ж)	[in'fɛktsiˈa]

66. Symptoms. Treatments. Part 3

hospital	лікарня (ж)	[liˈkarnˈa]
patient	пацієнт (ч)	[paˈtsiˈɛnt]
diagnosis	діагноз (ч)	[di'aɦnɔz]
cure	лікування (с)	[liku'wanˈa]
medical treatment	лікування (с)	[liku'wanˈa]
to get treatment	лікуватися	[liku'watisˈa]
to treat (~ a patient)	лікувати	[liku'wati]
to nurse (look after)	доглядати	[doɦlˈa'dati]
care (nursing ~)	догляд (ч)	['dɔɦlˈad]
operation, surgery	операція (ж)	[opɛ'ratsiˈa]
to bandage (head, limb)	перев'язати	[pɛrɛw'ˈa'zati]
bandaging	перев'язка (ж)	[pɛrɛ'wˈazka]
vaccination	щеплення (с)	['ɕɛplɛnˈa]
to vaccinate (vt)	робити щеплення	[ro'biti 'ɕɛplɛnˈa]
injection	ін'єкція (ж)	[i'nˈɛktsiˈa]
to give an injection	робити укол	[ro'biti u'kɔl]
amputation	ампутація (ж)	[ampu'tatsiˈa]
to amputate (vt)	ампутувати	[amputu'wati]
coma	кома (ж)	['kɔma]
to be in a coma	бути в комі	['buti w 'kɔmi]
intensive care	реанімація (ж)	[rɛani'matsiˈa]
to recover (~ from flu)	видужувати	[wiˈduʒuwati]
condition (patient's ~)	стан (ч)	['stan]
consciousness	свідомість (ж)	[swiˈdɔmistˈ]
memory (faculty)	пам'ять (ж)	['pamˈˈatˈ]
to pull out (tooth)	видалити	['widaliti]
filling	пломба (ж)	['plɔmba]
to fill (a tooth)	пломбувати	[plombu'wati]
hypnosis	гіпноз (ч)	[ɦip'nɔz]
to hypnotize (vt)	гіпнотизувати	[ɦipnotizu'wati]

67. Medicine. Drugs. Accessories

medicine, drug	ліки (мн)	['liki]
remedy	засіб (ч)	['zasib]
to prescribe (vt)	прописати	[propi'sati]
prescription	рецепт (ч)	[rɛ'tsɛpt]
tablet, pill	пігулка (ж)	[pi'ɦulka]

ointment	мазь (ж)	[mazʲ]
ampoule	ампула (ж)	['ampula]
mixture, solution	мікстура (ж)	[miks'tura]
syrup	сироп (ч)	[si'rɔp]
capsule	пілюля (ж)	[pi'lʲulʲa]
powder	порошок (ч)	[poro'ʃɔk]

gauze bandage	бинт (ч)	[bɨnt]
cotton wool	вата (ж)	['wata]
iodine	йод (ч)	[ʲod]

plaster	лейкопластир (ч)	[lɛjko'plastɨr]
eyedropper	піпетка (ж)	[pi'pɛtka]
thermometer	градусник (ч)	['ɦradusnɨk]
syringe	шприц (ч)	[ʃprɨts]

| wheelchair | коляска (ж) | [ko'lʲaska] |
| crutches | милиці (мн) | ['mɨlɨtsi] |

painkiller	знеболювальне (с)	[znɛ'bɔlʲuwalʲnɛ]
laxative	проносне (с)	[pronos'nɛ]
spirits (ethanol)	спирт (ч)	[spɨrt]
medicinal herbs	трава (ж)	[tra'wa]
herbal (~ tea)	трав'яний	[trawʲʲa'nɨj]

FLAT

flat	квартира (ж)	[kwar'tɨra]
room	кімната (ж)	[kim'nata]
bedroom	спальня (ж)	['spalʲnʲa]
dining room	їдальня (ж)	['jidalʲnʲa]
living room	вітальня (ж)	[wi'talʲnʲa]
study (home office)	кабінет (ч)	[kabi'nɛt]
entry room	передпокій (ч)	[pɛrɛd'pɔkij]
bathroom	ванна кімната (ж)	['wana kim'nata]
water closet	туалет (ч)	[tua'lɛt]
ceiling	стеля (ж)	['stɛlʲa]
floor	підлога (ж)	[pid'lɔɦa]
corner	куток (ч)	[ku'tɔk]

furniture	меблі (мн)	['mɛbli]
table	стіл (ч)	[stil]
chair	стілець (ч)	[sti'lɛts]
bed	ліжко (с)	['liʒko]
sofa, settee	диван (ч)	[di'wan]
armchair	крісло (с)	['krislo]
bookcase	шафа (ж)	['ʃafa]
shelf	полиця (ж)	[po'lɨtsʲa]
wardrobe	шафа (ж)	['ʃafa]
coat rack (wall-mounted ~)	вішалка (ж)	['wiʃalka]
coat stand	вішак (ч)	[wi'ʃak]
chest of drawers	комод (ч)	[ko'mɔd]
coffee table	журнальний столик (ч)	[ʒur'nalʲnij 'stɔlik]
mirror	дзеркало (с)	['dzɛrkalo]
carpet	килим (ч)	['kɨlɨm]
small carpet	килимок (ч)	[kɨlɨ'mɔk]
fireplace	камін (ч)	[ka'min]
candle	свічка (ж)	['switʃka]
candlestick	свічник (ч)	[switʃ'nik]
drapes	штори (мн)	['ʃtɔri]
wallpaper	шпалери (мн)	[ʃpa'lɛri]

blinds (jalousie)	жалюзі (мн)	['ʒalʲuzi]
table lamp	настільна лампа (ж)	[na'stilʲna 'lampa]
wall lamp (sconce)	світильник (ч)	[swi'tilʲnik]
standard lamp	торшер (ч)	[tor'ʃɛr]
chandelier	люстра (ж)	['lʲustra]

leg (of a chair, table)	ніжка (ж)	['niʒka]
armrest	підлокітник (ч)	[pidlo'kitnik]
back (backrest)	спинка (ж)	['spinka]
drawer	шухляда (ж)	[ʃuh'lʲada]

70. Bedding

bedclothes	білизна (ж)	[bi'lizna]
pillow	подушка (ж)	[po'duʃka]
pillowslip	наволочка (ж)	['nawolotʃka]
duvet	ковдра (ж)	['kɔwdra]
sheet	простирадло (с)	[prostiʲ'radlo]
bedspread	покривало (с)	[pokriʲ'walo]

71. Kitchen

kitchen	кухня (ж)	['kuhnʲa]
gas	газ (ч)	[ɦaz]
gas cooker	плита (ж) газова	[pli'ta 'ɦazowa]
electric cooker	плита (ж) електрична	[pli'ta ɛlɛkt'ritʃna]
oven	духовка (ж)	[du'hɔwka]
microwave oven	мікрохвильова піч (ж)	[mikrohwilʲo'wa pitʃ]

refrigerator	холодильник (ч)	[holo'dilʲnik]
freezer	морозильник (ч)	[moro'zilʲnik]
dishwasher	посудомийна машина (ж)	[posudo'mijna ma'ʃina]

mincer	м'ясорубка (ж)	[mʲaso'rubka]
juicer	соковижималка (ж)	[sokowiʒi'malka]
toaster	тостер (ч)	['tɔstɛr]
mixer	міксер (ч)	['miksɛr]

coffee machine	кавоварка (ж)	[kawo'warka]
coffee pot	кавник (ч)	[kaw'nik]
coffee grinder	кавомолка (ж)	[kawo'mɔlka]

kettle	чайник (ч)	['tʃajnik]
teapot	заварник (ч)	[za'warnik]
lid	кришка (ж)	['kriʃka]
tea strainer	ситечко (с)	['sitɛtʃko]

spoon	ложка (ж)	['lɔʒka]
teaspoon	чайна ложка (ж)	['tʃajna 'lɔʒka]
soup spoon	столова ложка (ж)	[sto'lowa 'lɔʒka]
fork	виделка (ж)	[wiʲ'dɛlka]
knife	ніж (ч)	[niʒ]

tableware (dishes)	посуд (ч)	['pɔsud]
plate (dinner ~)	тарілка (ж)	[ta'rilka]
saucer	блюдце (с)	['blʲudtsɛ]
shot glass	чарка (ж)	['tʃarka]
glass (tumbler)	склянка (ж)	['sklʲanka]
cup	чашка (ж)	['tʃaʃka]
sugar bowl	цукорниця (ж)	['tsukornitsʲa]
salt cellar	сільничка (ж)	[silʲ'nitʃka]
pepper pot	перечниця (ж)	['pɛrɛtʃnitsʲa]
butter dish	маслянка (ж)	['maslʲanka]
stock pot (soup pot)	каструля (ж)	[kas'trulʲa]
frying pan (skillet)	сковорідка (ж)	[skowo'ridka]
ladle	черпак (ч)	[tʃɛr'pak]
colander	друшляк (ч)	[druʃ'lʲak]
tray (serving ~)	піднос (ч)	[pid'nɔs]
bottle	пляшка (ж)	['plʲaʃka]
jar (glass)	банка (ж)	['banka]
tin (can)	банка (ж)	['banka]
bottle opener	відкривачка (ж)	[widkri'watʃka]
tin opener	відкривачка (ж)	[widkri'watʃka]
corkscrew	штопор (ч)	['ʃtopor]
filter	фільтр (ч)	['filʲtr]
to filter (vt)	фільтрувати	[filʲtru'wati]
waste (food ~, etc.)	сміття (с)	[smit'tʲa]
waste bin (kitchen ~)	відро (с) для сміття	[wid'ro dlʲa smit'tʲa]

72. Bathroom

bathroom	ванна кімната (ж)	['wana kim'nata]
water	вода (ж)	[wo'da]
tap	кран (ч)	[kran]
hot water	гаряча вода (ж)	[ɦa'rʲatʃa wo'da]
cold water	холодна вода (ж)	[ho'lɔdna wo'da]
toothpaste	зубна паста (ж)	[zub'na 'pasta]
to clean one's teeth	чистити зуби	['tʃistiti 'zubi]
to shave (vi)	голитися	[ɦo'litisʲa]
shaving foam	піна (ж) для гоління	['pina dlʲa ɦo'linʲa]
razor	бритва (ж)	['britwa]
to wash (one's hands, etc.)	мити	['miti]
to have a bath	митися	['mitisʲa]
shower	душ (ч)	[duʃ]
to have a shower	приймати душ	[prij'mati duʃ]
bath	ванна (ж)	['wana]
toilet (toilet bowl)	унітаз (ч)	[uni'taz]

sink (washbasin)	раковина (ж)	['rakowina]
soap	мило (c)	['miło]
soap dish	мильниця (ж)	['milʲnitsʲa]

sponge	губка (ж)	['ĥubka]
shampoo	шампунь (ч)	[ʃam'punʲ]
towel	рушник (ч)	[ruʃ'nik]
bathrobe	халат (ч)	[ha'lat]

laundry (laundering)	прання (c)	[pra'nʲa]
washing machine	пральна машина (ж)	['pralʲna ma'ʃina]
to do the laundry	прати білизну	['prati bi'liznu]
washing powder	пральний порошок (ч)	['pralʲnij poro'ʃok]

73. Household appliances

TV, telly	телевізор (ч)	[tɛlɛ'wizor]
tape recorder	магнітофон (ч)	[maĥnito'fɔn]
video	відеомагнітофон (ч)	['widɛo maĥnito'fɔn]
radio	приймач (ч)	[prij'matʃ]
player (CD, MP3, etc.)	плеєр (ч)	['plɛɛr]

video projector	відеопроектор (ч)	['widɛo pro'ɛktor]
home cinema	домашній кінотеатр (ч)	[do'maʃnij kinotɛ'atr]
DVD player	програвач (ч) DVD	[proĥra'watʃ diwi'di]
amplifier	підсилювач (ч)	[pid'silʲuwatʃ]
video game console	гральна приставка (ж)	['ĥralʲna pri'stawka]

video camera	відеокамера (ж)	['widɛo 'kamɛra]
camera (photo)	фотоапарат (ч)	[fotoapa'rat]
digital camera	цифровий фотоапарат (ч)	[tsifro'wij fotoapa'rat]

vacuum cleaner	пилосос (ч)	[piło'sɔs]
iron (e.g. steam ~)	праска (ж)	['praska]
ironing board	дошка (ж) для прасування	['dɔʃka dlʲa prasu'wanʲa]

telephone	телефон (ч)	[tɛlɛ'fɔn]
mobile phone	мобільний телефон (ч)	[mo'bilʲnij tɛlɛ'fɔn]
typewriter	машинка (ж)	[ma'ʃinka]
sewing machine	швейна машинка (ж)	['ʃwɛjna ma'ʃinka]

microphone	мікрофон (ч)	[mikro'fɔn]
headphones	навушники (мн)	[na'wuʃniki]
remote control (TV)	пульт (ч)	[pulʲt]

CD, compact disc	CD-диск (ч)	[si'di disk]
cassette, tape	касета (ж)	[ka'sɛta]
vinyl record	платівка (ж)	[pla'tiwka]

THE EARTH. WEATHER

74. Outer space

space	космос (ч)	['kɔsmos]
space (as adj)	космічний	[kos'mitʃnij]
outer space	космічний простір (ч)	[kos'mitʃnij 'prɔstir]
world, universe	всесвіт (ч)	['wsɛswit]
galaxy	галактика (ж)	[ɦa'laktika]
star	зірка (ж)	['zirka]
constellation	сузір'я (с)	[su'zirʲʲa]
planet	планета (ж)	[pla'nɛta]
satellite	супутник (ч)	[su'putnik]
meteorite	метеорит (ч)	[mɛtɛo'rit]
comet	комета (ж)	[ko'mɛta]
asteroid	астероїд (ч)	[astɛ'rɔjid]
orbit	орбіта (ж)	[or'bita]
to revolve (~ around the Earth)	обертатися	[obɛr'tatisʲa]
atmosphere	атмосфера (ж)	[atmos'fɛra]
the Sun	Сонце (с)	['sɔntsɛ]
solar system	Сонячна система (ж)	['sɔnʲatʃna sis'tɛma]
solar eclipse	сонячне затемнення (с)	['sɔnʲatʃnɛ za'tɛmnɛnʲa]
the Earth	Земля (ж)	[zɛm'lʲa]
the Moon	Місяць (ж)	['misʲats]
Mars	Марс (ч)	[mars]
Venus	Венера (ж)	[wɛ'nɛra]
Jupiter	Юпітер (ч)	[ʲu'pitɛr]
Saturn	Сатурн (ч)	[sa'turn]
Mercury	Меркурій (ч)	[mɛr'kurij]
Uranus	Уран (ч)	[u'ran]
Neptune	Нептун (ч)	[nɛp'tun]
Pluto	Плутон (ч)	[plu'tɔn]
Milky Way	Чумацький Шлях (ч)	[tʃu'matskij ʃlʲah]
Great Bear (Ursa Major)	Велика Ведмедиця (ж)	[wɛ'lika wɛd'mɛditsʲa]
North Star	Полярна Зірка (ж)	[po'lʲarna 'zirka]
Martian	марсіанин (ч)	[marsi'anin]
extraterrestrial (n)	інопланетянин (ч)	[inoplanɛ'tʲanin]
alien	прибулець (ч)	[pri'bulɛts]

flying saucer	літальна тарілка (ж)	[li'talʲna ta'rilka]
spaceship	космічний корабель (ч)	[kos'mitʃnij kora'bɛlʲ]
space station	орбітальна станція (ж)	[orbi'talʲna 'stantsiʲa]
blast-off	старт (ч)	[start]

engine	двигун (ч)	[dwi'ɦun]
nozzle	сопло (с)	['sɔplo]
fuel	паливо (с)	['paliwo]

| cockpit, flight deck | кабіна (ж) | [ka'bina] |
| aerial | антена (ж) | [an'tɛna] |

porthole	ілюмінатор (ч)	[ilʲumi'nator]
solar panel	сонячна батарея (ж)	['sɔnʲatʃna bata'rɛʲa]
spacesuit	скафандр (ч)	[ska'fandr]

| weightlessness | невагомість (ж) | [nɛwa'ɦomistʲ] |
| oxygen | кисень (ч) | ['kisɛnʲ] |

| docking (in space) | стикування (с) | [stiku'wanʲa] |
| to dock (vi, vt) | здійснювати стикування | ['zdijsnʲuwati stiku'wanʲa] |

| observatory | обсерваторія (ж) | [obsɛrwa'toriʲa] |
| telescope | телескоп (ч) | [tɛlɛ'skɔp] |

| to observe (vt) | спостерігати | [spostɛri'ɦati] |
| to explore (vt) | досліджувати | [do'slidʒuwati] |

75. The Earth

the Earth	Земля (ж)	[zɛm'lʲa]
the globe (the Earth)	земна куля (ж)	[zɛm'na 'kulʲa]
planet	планета (ж)	[pla'nɛta]

atmosphere	атмосфера (ж)	[atmos'fɛra]
geography	географія (ж)	[ɦɛo'ɦrafiʲa]
nature	природа (ж)	[pri'rɔda]

globe (table ~)	глобус (ч)	['ɦlobus]
map	карта (ж)	['karta]
atlas	атлас (ч)	['atlas]

| Europe | Європа (ж) | [ɛw'rɔpa] |
| Asia | Азія (ж) | ['aziʲa] |

| Africa | Африка (ж) | ['afrika] |
| Australia | Австралія (ж) | [aw'straliʲa] |

America	Америка (ж)	[a'mɛrika]
North America	Північна Америка (ж)	[piw'nitʃna a'mɛrika]
South America	Південна Америка (ж)	[piw'dɛna a'mɛrika]

| Antarctica | Антарктида (ж) | [antark'tida] |
| the Arctic | Арктика (ж) | ['arktika] |

76. Cardinal directions

north	північ (ж)	['piwnitʃ]
to the north	на північ	[na 'piwnitʃ]
in the north	на півночі	[na 'piwnotʃi]
northern (adj)	північний	[piw'nitʃnij]

south	південь (ч)	['piwdɛnʲ]
to the south	на південь	[na 'piwdɛnʲ]
in the south	на півдні	[na 'piwdni]
southern (adj)	південний	[piw'dɛnij]

west	захід (ч)	['zahid]
to the west	на захід	[na 'zahid]
in the west	на заході	[na 'zahodi]
western (adj)	західний	['zahidnij]

east	схід (ч)	[shid]
to the east	на схід	[na 'shid]
in the east	на сході	[na 'shɔdi]
eastern (adj)	східний	['shidnij]

77. Sea. Ocean

sea	море (с)	['mɔrɛ]
ocean	океан (ч)	[okɛ'an]
gulf (bay)	затока (ж)	[za'tɔka]
straits	протока (ж)	[pro'tɔka]

continent (mainland)	материк (ч)	[matɛ'rik]
island	острів (ч)	['ɔstriw]
peninsula	півострів (ч)	[pi'wɔstriw]
archipelago	архіпелаг (ч)	[arhipɛ'lañ]

bay, cove	бухта (ж)	['buhta]
harbour	гавань (ж)	['ñawanʲ]
lagoon	лагуна (ж)	[la'ñuna]
cape	мис (ч)	[mis]

atoll	атол (ч)	[a'tɔl]
reef	риф (ч)	[rif]
coral	корал (ч)	[ko'ral]
coral reef	кораловий риф (ч)	[ko'ralowij rif]

deep (adj)	глибокий	[ñlï'bokij]
depth (deep water)	глибина (ж)	[ñlïbï'na]
abyss	бездна (ж)	['bɛzdna]
trench (e.g. Mariana ~)	западина (ж)	[za'padina]

current (Ocean ~)	течія (ж)	['tɛtʃʲʲa]
to surround (bathe)	омивати	[omiʲwati]
shore	берег (ч)	['bɛrɛñ]
coast	узбережжя (с)	[uzbɛ'rɛzʲa]

flow (flood tide)	приплив (ч)	[prip'liw]
ebb (ebb tide)	відплив (ч)	[wid'pliw]
shoal	обмілина (ж)	[ob'milina]
bottom (~ of the sea)	дно (с)	[dno]
wave	хвиля (ж)	['hwilʲa]
crest (~ of a wave)	гребінь (ч) хвилі	['ɦrɛbinʲ 'hwili]
spume (sea foam)	піна (ж)	[pi'na]
storm (sea storm)	буря (ж)	['burʲa]
hurricane	ураган (ч)	[uraɦan]
tsunami	цунамі (с)	[tsu'nami]
calm (dead ~)	штиль (ч)	[ʃtilʲ]
quiet, calm (adj)	спокійний	[spo'kijnij]
pole	полюс (ч)	['polʲus]
polar (adj)	полярний	[po'lʲarnij]
latitude	широта (ж)	[ʃiro'ta]
longitude	довгота (ж)	[dowɦo'ta]
parallel	паралель (ж)	[para'lɛlʲ]
equator	екватор (ч)	[ɛk'wator]
sky	небо (с)	['nɛbo]
horizon	горизонт (ч)	[ɦori'zɔnt]
air	повітря (с)	[po'witrʲa]
lighthouse	маяк (ч)	[ma'ʲak]
to dive (vi)	пірнати	[pir'nati]
to sink (ab. boat)	затонути	[zato'nuti]
treasure	скарби (мн)	[skar'bi]

78. Seas & Oceans names

Atlantic Ocean	Атлантичний океан (ч)	[atlan'titʃnij okɛ'an]
Indian Ocean	Індійський океан (ч)	[in'dijsʲkij okɛ'an]
Pacific Ocean	Тихий океан (ч)	['tiɦij okɛ'an]
Arctic Ocean	Північний Льодовитий океан (ч)	[piw'nitʃnij lʲodo'witij okɛ'an]
Black Sea	Чорне море (с)	['tʃɔrnɛ 'mɔrɛ]
Red Sea	Червоне море (с)	[tʃɛr'wonɛ 'mɔrɛ]
Yellow Sea	Жовте море (с)	['ʒowtɛ 'mɔrɛ]
White Sea	Біле море (с)	['bilɛ 'mɔrɛ]
Caspian Sea	Каспійське море (с)	[kas'pijsʲkɛ 'mɔrɛ]
Dead Sea	Мертве море (с)	['mɛrtwɛ 'mɔrɛ]
Mediterranean Sea	Середземне море (с)	[sɛrɛ'dzɛmnɛ 'mɔrɛ]
Aegean Sea	Егейське море (с)	[ɛ'ɦɛjsʲkɛ 'mɔrɛ]
Adriatic Sea	Адріатичне море (с)	[adria'titʃnɛ 'mɔrɛ]
Arabian Sea	Аравійське море (с)	[ara'wijsʲkɛ 'mɔrɛ]
Sea of Japan	Японське море (с)	[ja'ponsʲkɛ 'mɔrɛ]

| Bering Sea | Берингове море (с) | ['bɛrinɦowɛ 'mɔrɛ] |
| South China Sea | Південно-Китайське море (с) | [piw'dɛno ki'tajsʲkɛ 'mɔrɛ] |

Coral Sea	Коралове море (с)	[ko'ralowɛ 'mɔrɛ]
Tasman Sea	Тасманове море (с)	[tas'manowɛ 'mɔrɛ]
Caribbean Sea	Карибське море (с)	[ka'ribsʲkɛ 'mɔrɛ]

| Barents Sea | Баренцове море (с) | ['barɛntsowɛ 'mɔrɛ] |
| Kara Sea | Карське море (с) | ['karsʲkɛ 'mɔrɛ] |

North Sea	Північне море (с)	[piw'nitʃɛ 'mɔrɛ]
Baltic Sea	Балтійське море (с)	[bal'tijsʲkɛ 'mɔrɛ]
Norwegian Sea	Норвезьке море (с)	[nor'wɛzʲkɛ 'mɔrɛ]

79. Mountains

mountain	гора (ж)	[ɦo'ra]
mountain range	гірське пасмо (с)	[ɦirsʲ'kɛ 'pasmo]
mountain ridge	гірський хребет (ч)	[ɦirsʲ'kij ɦrɛ'bɛt]

summit, top	вершина (ж)	[wɛr'ʃina]
peak	шпиль (ч)	[ʃpilʲ]
foot (~ of the mountain)	підніжжя (с)	[pid'nizʲa]
slope (mountainside)	схил (ч)	[sɦil]

volcano	вулкан (ч)	[wul'kan]
active volcano	діючий вулкан (ч)	['diʲutʃij wul'kan]
dormant volcano	згаслий вулкан (ч)	['zɦaslij wul'kan]

eruption	виверження (с)	['wiwɛrʒɛnʲa]
crater	кратер (ч)	['kratɛr]
magma	магма (ж)	['maɦma]
lava	лава (ж)	['lawa]
molten (~ lava)	розжарений	[roz'ʒarɛnij]

canyon	каньйон (ч)	[kanʲ'jɔn]
gorge	ущелина (ж)	[u'ɕɛlina]
crevice	ущелина (с)	[u'ɕɛlina]

pass, col	перевал (ч)	[pɛrɛ'wal]
plateau	плато (с)	['plato]
cliff	скеля (ж)	['skɛlʲa]
hill	горб (ч)	[ɦorb]

glacier	льодовик (ч)	[lʲodo'wik]
waterfall	водоспад (ч)	[wodos'pad]
geyser	гейзер (ч)	['ɦejzɛr]
lake	озеро (с)	['ɔzɛro]

plain	рівнина (ж)	[riw'nina]
landscape	краєвид (ч)	[kraɛ'wid]
echo	луна (ж)	[lu'na]
alpinist	альпініст (ч)	[alʲpi'nist]

rock climber	скелелаз (ч)	[skɛlɛ'laz]
to conquer (in climbing)	підкоряти	[pidko'rʲati]
climb (an easy ~)	піднімання (с)	[pidni'manʲa]

80. Mountains names

The Alps	Альпи (мн)	['alʲpi]
Mont Blanc	Монблан (ч)	[mon'blan]
The Pyrenees	Піренеї (мн)	[pirɛ'nɛjі]
The Carpathians	Карпати (мн)	[kar'pati]
The Ural Mountains	Уральські гори (мн)	[u'ralʲsʲki 'ɦori]
The Caucasus Mountains	Кавказ (ч)	[kaw'kaz]
Mount Elbrus	Ельбрус (ч)	[ɛlʲb'rus]
The Altai Mountains	Алтай (ч)	[al'taj]
The Tian Shan	Тянь-Шань (мн)	[tʲanʲ 'ʃanʲ]
The Pamirs	Памір (ч)	[pa'mir]
The Himalayas	Гімалаї (мн)	[ɦima'laji]
Mount Everest	Еверест (ч)	[ɛwɛ'rɛst]
The Andes	Анди (мн)	['andi]
Mount Kilimanjaro	Кіліманджаро (ж)	[kiliman'dʒaro]

81. Rivers

river	ріка (ж)	['rika]
spring (natural source)	джерело (с)	[dʒɛrɛ'lɔ]
riverbed (river channel)	річище (с)	['ritʃiɕɛ]
basin (river valley)	басейн (ч)	[ba'sɛjn]
to flow into ...	упадати	[upa'dati]
tributary	притока (ж)	[pri'tɔka]
bank (river ~)	берег (ч)	['bɛrɛɦ]
current (stream)	течія (ж)	['tɛtʃʲʲa]
downstream (adv)	вниз за течією (ж)	[wniz za 'tɛtʃiɛʲu]
upstream (adv)	уверх по течії	[u'wɛrh po 'tɛtʃiji]
inundation	повінь (ж)	['powinʲ]
flooding	повінь (ж)	['powinʲ]
to overflow (vi)	розливатися	[rozli'watisʲa]
to flood (vt)	затоплювати	[za'tɔplʲuwati]
shallow (shoal)	мілина (ж)	[mili'na]
rapids	поріг (ч)	[po'riɦ]
dam	гребля (ж)	['ɦrɛblʲa]
canal	канал (ч)	[ka'nal]
reservoir (artificial lake)	водосховище (с)	[wodo'showiɕɛ]
sluice, lock	шлюз (ч)	[ʃlʲuz]
water body (pond, etc.)	водоймище (с)	[wo'dojmiɕɛ]

swamp (marshland)	болото (с)	[bo'loto]
bog, marsh	трясовина (ж)	[trʲasowi'na]
whirlpool	вир (ч)	[wir]

stream (brook)	струмок (ч)	[stru'mɔk]
drinking (ab. water)	питний	['pitnij]
fresh (~ water)	прісний	['prisnij]

| ice | крига (ж) | ['kriɦa] |
| to freeze over (ab. river, etc.) | замерзнути | [za'mɛrznutɪ] |

82. Rivers names

| Seine | Сена (ж) | ['sɛna] |
| Loire | Луара (ж) | [lu'ara] |

Thames	Темза (ж)	['tɛmza]
Rhine	Рейн (ч)	[rɛjn]
Danube	Дунай (ч)	[du'naj]

Volga	Волга (ж)	['wɔlɦa]
Don	Дон (ч)	[don]
Lena	Лена (ж)	['lɛna]

Yellow River	Хуанхе (ж)	[huan'hɛ]
Yangtze	Янцзи (ж)	[janʦ'zi]
Mekong	Меконг (ч)	[mɛ'kɔnɦ]
Ganges	Ганг (ч)	[ɦanɦ]

Nile River	Ніл (ч)	[nil]
Congo River	Конго (ж)	['kɔnɦo]
Okavango River	Окаванго (ж)	[oka'wanɦo]
Zambezi River	Замбезі (ж)	[zam'bɛzi]
Limpopo River	Лімпопо (ж)	[limpo'pɔ]
Mississippi River	Міссісіпі (ж)	[misi'sipi]

83. Forest

| forest, wood | ліс (ч) | [lis] |
| forest (as adj) | лісовий | [liso'wij] |

thick forest	хаща (ж)	['haɕa]
grove	гай (ч)	[ɦaj]
forest clearing	галявина (ж)	[ɦa'lʲawina]

| thicket | хащі (мн) | ['haɕi] |
| scrubland | чагарник (ч) | [ʧa'ɦarnik] |

footpath (troddenpath)	стежина (ж)	[stɛ'ʒina]
gully	яр (ч)	[jar]
tree	дерево (с)	['dɛrɛwo]
leaf	листок (ч)	[lɪs'tɔk]

leaves (foliage)	листя (с)	['listʲa]
fall of leaves	листопад (ч)	[listo'pad]
to fall (ab. leaves)	опадати	[opa'dati]
top (of the tree)	верхівка (ж)	[wɛr'hiwka]

branch	гілка (ж)	['ɦilka]
bough	сук (ч)	[suk]
bud (on shrub, tree)	брунька (ж)	['brunʲka]
needle (of the pine tree)	голка (ж)	['ɦɔlka]
fir cone	шишка (ж)	['ʃiʃka]

tree hollow	дупло (с)	[dup'lɔ]
nest	гніздо (с)	[ɦniz'dɔ]
burrow (animal hole)	нора (ж)	[no'ra]

trunk	стовбур (ч)	['stɔwbur]
root	корінь (ч)	['korinʲ]
bark	кора (ж)	[ko'ra]
moss	мох (ч)	[moh]

to uproot (remove trees or tree stumps)	корчувати	[kortʃu'wati]
to chop down	рубати	[ru'bati]
to deforest (vt)	вирубувати	[wi'rubuwati]
tree stump	пень (ч)	[pɛnʲ]

campfire	багаття (с)	[ba'ɦattʲa]
forest fire	пожежа (ж)	[po'ʒɛʒa]
to extinguish (vt)	тушити	[tu'ʃiti]

forest ranger	лісник (ч)	[lis'nik]
protection	охорона (ж)	[oho'rona]
to protect (~ nature)	охороняти	[ohoro'nʲati]
poacher	браконьєр (ч)	[brako'nʲɛr]
steel trap	пастка (ж)	['pastka]

| to gather, to pick (vt) | збирати | [zbi'rati] |
| to lose one's way | заблукати | [zablu'kati] |

84. Natural resources

natural resources	природні ресурси (мн)	[pri'rɔdni rɛ'sursi]
minerals	корисні копалини (мн)	['kɔrisni ko'palini]
deposits	поклади (мн)	['pɔkladi]
field (e.g. oilfield)	родовище (с)	[ro'dɔwiɕɛ]

to mine (extract)	добувати	[dobu'wati]
mining (extraction)	добування (с)	[dobu'wanʲa]
ore	руда (ж)	[ru'da]
mine (e.g. for coal)	копальня (ж)	[ko'palʲnʲa]
shaft (mine ~)	шахта (ж)	['ʃahta]
miner	шахтар (ч)	[ʃah'tar]
gas (natural ~)	газ (ч)	[ɦaz]
gas pipeline	газопровід (ч)	[ɦazopro'wid]

oil (petroleum)	нафта (ж)	['nafta]
oil pipeline	нафтопровід (ч)	[nafto'prɔwid]
oil well	нафтова вишка (ж)	['naftowa 'wiʃka]
derrick (tower)	свердлова вежа (ж)	[swɛrd'lɔwa 'wɛʒa]
tanker	танкер (ч)	['tankɛr]

sand	пісок (ч)	[pi'sɔk]
limestone	вапняк (ч)	[wap'nʲak]
gravel	гравій (ч)	['ɦrawij]
peat	торф (ч)	[torf]
clay	глина (ж)	['ɦlina]
coal	вугілля (с)	[wu'ɦilʲa]

iron (ore)	залізо (с)	[za'lizo]
gold	золото (с)	['zɔloto]
silver	срібло (с)	['sriblo]
nickel	нікель (ч)	['nikɛlʲ]
copper	мідь (ж)	[midʲ]

zinc	цинк (ч)	['ʦink]
manganese	марганець (ч)	['marɦanɛʦ]
mercury	ртуть (ж)	[rtutʲ]
lead	свинець (ч)	[swi'nɛʦ]

mineral	мінерал (ч)	[minɛ'ral]
crystal	кристал (ч)	[kris'tal]
marble	мармур (ч)	['marmur]
uranium	уран (ч)	[u'ran]

85. Weather

weather	погода (ж)	[po'ɦoda]
weather forecast	прогноз (ч) погоди (ж)	[proɦ'nɔz po'ɦodi]
temperature	температура (ж)	[tɛmpɛra'tura]
thermometer	термометр (ч)	[tɛr'mɔmɛtr]
barometer	барометр (ч)	[ba'rɔmɛtr]

humidity	вологість (ж)	[woloɦistʲ]
heat (extreme ~)	спека (ж)	['spɛka]
hot (torrid)	гарячий	[ɦa'rʲatʃij]
it's hot	спекотно	[spɛ'kɔtno]

| it's warm | тепло | ['tɛplo] |
| warm (moderately hot) | теплий | ['tɛplij] |

| it's cold | холодно | ['hɔlodno] |
| cold (adj) | холодний | [ho'lɔdnij] |

sun	сонце (с)	['sɔnʦɛ]
to shine (vi)	світити	[swi'titi]
sunny (day)	сонячний	['sɔnʲatʃnij]
to come up (vi)	зійти	[zij'ti]
to set (vi)	сісти	['sisti]
cloud	хмара (ж)	['hmara]

cloudy (adj)	хмарний	['hmarnij]
rain cloud	хмара (ж)	['hmara]
somber (gloomy)	похмурний	[poh'murnij]

rain	дощ (ч)	[doɕ]
it's raining	йде дощ	[jdɛ doɕ]
rainy (~ day, weather)	дощовий	[doɕo'wij]
to drizzle (vi)	накрапати	[nakra'pati]

pouring rain	проливний дощ (ч)	[proliw'nij doɕ]
downpour	злива (ж)	['zɫiwa]
heavy (e.g. ~ rain)	сильний	['siɫ'nij]
puddle	калюжа (ж)	[ka'lʲuʒa]
to get wet (in rain)	мокнути	['mɔknuti]

fog (mist)	туман (ч)	[tu'man]
foggy	туманний	[tu'manij]
snow	сніг (ч)	[sniɦ]
it's snowing	йде сніг (ч)	[jdɛ sniɦ]

86. Severe weather. Natural disasters

thunderstorm	гроза (ж)	[ɦro'za]
lightning (~ strike)	блискавка (ж)	['bliskawka]
to flash (vi)	блискати	['bliskati]

thunder	грім (ч)	[ɦrim]
to thunder (vi)	гриміти	[ɦri'miti]
it's thundering	гримить грім	[ɦri'mitʲ ɦrim]

| hail | град (ч) | [ɦrad] |
| it's hailing | йде град | [jdɛ ɦrad] |

| to flood (vt) | затопити | [zato'piti] |
| flood, inundation | повінь (ж) | ['pɔwinʲ] |

earthquake	землетрус (ч)	[zɛmlɛt'rus]
tremor, shoke	поштовх (ч)	['pɔʃtowɦ]
epicentre	епіцентр (ч)	[ɛpi'ʦɛntr]

| eruption | виверження (с) | ['wiwɛrʒɛnʲa] |
| lava | лава (ж) | ['lawa] |

twister	смерч (ч)	[smɛrʧ]
tornado	торнадо (ч)	[tor'nado]
typhoon	тайфун (ч)	[taj'fun]

hurricane	ураган (ч)	[uraɦan]
storm	буря (ж)	['burʲa]
tsunami	цунамі (с)	[ʦu'nami]

cyclone	циклон (ч)	[ʦik'lɔn]
bad weather	негода (ж)	[nɛ'ɦoda]
fire (accident)	пожежа (ж)	[po'ʒɛʒa]

disaster	катастрофа (ж)	[kata'strofa]
meteorite	метеорит (ч)	[mɛtɛo'rit]
avalanche	лавина (ж)	[la'wina]
snowslide	обвал (ч)	[ob'wal]
blizzard	заметіль (ж)	[zamɛ'tilʲ]
snowstorm	завірюха (ж)	[zawi'rʲuha]

FAUNA

predator	хижак (ч)	[hi'ʒak]
tiger	тигр (ч)	[tiɦr]
lion	лев (ч)	[lɛw]
wolf	вовк (ч)	[wowk]
fox	лисиця (ж)	[lɨ'sʲitsʲa]
jaguar	ягуар (ч)	[jaɦu'ar]
leopard	леопард (ч)	[lɛo'pard]
cheetah	гепард (ч)	[ɦɛ'pard]
black panther	пантера (ж)	[pan'tɛra]
puma	пума (ж)	['puma]
snow leopard	сніговий барс (ч)	[sniɦo'wij bars]
lynx	рись (ж)	[risʲ]
coyote	койот (ч)	[ko'jot]
jackal	шакал (ч)	[ʃa'kal]
hyena	гієна (ж)	[ɦi'ɛna]

animal	тварина (ж)	[twa'rɨna]
beast (animal)	звір (ч)	[zwir]
squirrel	білка (ж)	['bilka]
hedgehog	їжак (ч)	[ji'ʒak]
hare	заєць (ч)	['zaɛts]
rabbit	кріль (ч)	[krilʲ]
badger	борсук (ч)	[bor'suk]
raccoon	єнот (ч)	[ɛ'nɔt]
hamster	хом'як (ч)	[ho'mʲak]
marmot	бабак (ч)	[ba'bak]
mole	кріт (ч)	[krit]
mouse	миша (ж)	['mɨʃa]
rat	щур (ч)	[ɕur]
bat	кажан (ч)	[ka'ʒan]
ermine	горностай (ч)	[ɦorno'staj]
sable	соболь (ч)	['sɔbolʲ]
marten	куниця (ж)	[ku'nɨtsʲa]
weasel	ласка (ж)	['laska]
mink	норка (ж)	['nɔrka]

| beaver | бобер (ч) | [bo'bεr] |
| otter | видра (ж) | ['wɨdra] |

horse	кінь (ч)	[kinʲ]
moose	лось (ч)	[losʲ]
deer	олень (ч)	['ɔlεnʲ]
camel	верблюд (ч)	[wεr'blʲud]

bison	бізон (ч)	[bi'zɔn]
wisent	зубр (ч)	[zubr]
buffalo	буйвіл (ч)	['bujwil]

zebra	зебра (ж)	['zεbra]
antelope	антилопа (ж)	[antɨ'lɔpa]
roe deer	косуля (ж)	[ko'sulʲa]
fallow deer	лань (ж)	[lanʲ]
chamois	сарна (ж)	['sarna]
wild boar	вепр (ч)	[wεpr]

whale	кит (ч)	[kɨt]
seal	тюлень (ч)	[tʲu'lεnʲ]
walrus	морж (ч)	[morʒ]
fur seal	котик (ч)	['kotik]
dolphin	дельфін (ч)	[dεlʲ'fin]

bear	ведмідь (ч)	[wεd'midʲ]
polar bear	білий ведмідь (ч)	['bilij wεd'midʲ]
panda	панда (ж)	['panda]

monkey	мавпа (ж)	['mawpa]
chimpanzee	шимпанзе (ч)	[ʃimpan'zε]
orangutan	орангутанг (ч)	[oranɦu'tanɦ]
gorilla	горила (ж)	[ɦo'rila]
macaque	макака (ж)	[ma'kaka]
gibbon	гібон (ч)	[ɦi'bɔn]

elephant	слон (ч)	[slon]
rhinoceros	носоріг (ч)	[noso'riɦ]
giraffe	жирафа (ж)	[ʒɨrafa]
hippopotamus	бегемот (ч)	[bεɦε'mɔt]

| kangaroo | кенгуру (ч) | [kεnɦu'ru] |
| koala (bear) | коала (ч) | [ko'ala] |

mongoose	мангуст (ч)	[ma'nɦust]
chinchilla	шиншила (ж)	[ʃin'ʃila]
skunk	скунс (ч)	[skuns]
porcupine	дикобраз (ч)	[diko'braz]

89. Domestic animals

cat	кішка (ж)	['kiʃka]
tomcat	кіт (ч)	[kit]
horse	коняка (ж)	[ko'nʲaka]

stallion (male horse)	жеребець (ч)	[ʒɛrɛˈbɛts]
mare	кобила (ж)	[koˈbila]
cow	корова (ж)	[koˈrɔwa]
bull	бик (ч)	[bɨk]
ox	віл (ч)	[wil]
sheep (ewe)	вівця (ж)	[wiwˈtsʲa]
ram	баран (ч)	[baˈran]
goat	коза (ж)	[koˈza]
billy goat, he-goat	козел (ч)	[koˈzɛl]
donkey	осел (ч)	[oˈsɛl]
mule	мул (ч)	[mul]
pig	свиня (ж)	[swiˈnʲa]
piglet	порося (с)	[poroˈsʲa]
rabbit	кріль (ч)	[krilʲ]
hen (chicken)	курка (ж)	[ˈkurka]
cock	півень (ч)	[ˈpiwɛnʲ]
duck	качка (ж)	[ˈkatʃka]
drake	качур (ч)	[ˈkatʃur]
goose	гусак (ч)	[ɦuˈsak]
tom turkey, gobbler	індик (ч)	[inˈdɨk]
turkey (hen)	індичка (ж)	[inˈdɨtʃka]
domestic animals	домашні тварини (мн)	[doˈmaʃni twaˈrɨni]
tame (e.g. ~ hamster)	ручний	[rutʃˈnij]
to tame (vt)	приручати	[priruˈtʃati]
to breed (vt)	вирощувати	[wiˈrɔɕuwati]
farm	ферма (ж)	[ˈfɛrma]
poultry	свійські птахи (мн)	[ˈswijsʲki ptaˈhi]
cattle	худоба (ж)	[ɦuˈdɔba]
herd (cattle)	стадо (с)	[ˈstado]
stable	конюшня (ж)	[koˈnʲuʃnʲa]
pigsty	свинарник (ч)	[swiˈnarnik]
cowshed	корівник (ч)	[koˈriwnik]
rabbit hutch	крільчатник (ч)	[krilʲˈtʃatnik]
hen house	курник (ч)	[kurˈnik]

90. Birds

bird	птах (ч)	[ptah]
pigeon	голуб (ч)	[ˈɦɔlub]
sparrow	горобець (ч)	[ɦoroˈbɛts]
tit (great tit)	синиця (ж)	[sɨˈnɨtsʲa]
magpie	сорока (ж)	[soˈrɔka]
raven	ворон (ч)	[ˈwɔron]
crow	ворона (ж)	[woˈrɔna]

| jackdaw | галка (ж) | ['ɦalka] |
| rook | грак (ч) | [ɦrak] |

duck	качка (ж)	['katʃka]
goose	гусак (ч)	[ɦu'sak]
pheasant	фазан (ч)	[fa'zan]

eagle	орел (ч)	[o'rɛl]
hawk	яструб (ч)	['ʲastrub]
falcon	сокіл (ч)	['sɔkil]
vulture	гриф (ч)	[ɦrif]
condor (Andean ~)	кондор (ч)	['kɔndor]

swan	лебідь (ч)	['lɛbidʲ]
crane	журавель (ч)	[ʒura'wɛlʲ]
stork	чорногуз (ч)	[tʃorno'ɦuz]

parrot	папуга (ч)	[pa'puɦa]
hummingbird	колібрі (ч)	[ko'libri]
peacock	пава (ж)	['pawa]

ostrich	страус (ч)	['straus]
heron	чапля (ж)	['tʃaplʲa]
flamingo	фламінго (с)	[fla'minɦo]
pelican	пелікан (ч)	[pɛli'kan]

| nightingale | соловей (ч) | [solo'wɛj] |
| swallow | ластівка (ж) | ['lastiwka] |

thrush	дрізд (ч)	[drizd]
song thrush	співучий дрізд (ч)	[spi'wutʃij 'drizd]
blackbird	чорний дрізд (ч)	['tʃornij 'drizd]

swift	стриж (ч)	['striʒ]
lark	жайворонок (ч)	['ʒajworonok]
quail	перепел (ч)	['pɛrɛpɛl]

woodpecker	дятел (ч)	['dʲatɛl]
cuckoo	зозуля (ж)	[zo'zulʲa]
owl	сова (ж)	[so'wa]
eagle owl	пугач (ч)	[pu'ɦatʃ]
wood grouse	глухар (ч)	[ɦlu'ɦar]

| black grouse | тетерук (ч) | [tɛtɛ'ruk] |
| partridge | куріпка (ж) | [ku'ripka] |

starling	шпак (ч)	[ʃpak]
canary	канарка (ж)	[ka'narka]
hazel grouse	рябчик (ч)	['rʲabtʃik]

| chaffinch | зяблик (ч) | ['zʲablik] |
| bullfinch | снігур (ч) | [sni'ɦur] |

seagull	чайка (ж)	['tʃajka]
albatross	альбатрос (ч)	[alʲbat'rɔs]
penguin	пінгвін (ч)	[pinɦ'win]

91. Fish. Marine animals

bream	лящ (ч)	[ˡˈaɕ]
carp	короп (ч)	[ˈkɔrop]
perch	окунь (ч)	[ˈɔkunʲ]
catfish	сом (ч)	[som]
pike	щука (ж)	[ˈɕuka]
salmon	лосось (ч)	[loˈsɔsʲ]
sturgeon	осетер (ч)	[osɛˈtɛr]
herring	оселедець (ч)	[osɛˈlɛdɛʦ]
Atlantic salmon	сьомга (ж)	[ˈsʲomɦa]
mackerel	скумбрія (ж)	[ˈskumbriʲa]
flatfish	камбала (ж)	[kambaˈla]
zander, pike perch	судак (ч)	[suˈdak]
cod	тріска (ж)	[trisˈka]
tuna	тунець (ч)	[tuˈnɛʦ]
trout	форель (ж)	[foˈrɛlʲ]
eel	вугор (ч)	[wuˈɦɔr]
electric ray	електричний скат (ч)	[ɛlɛktˈriʧnij skat]
moray eel	мурена (ж)	[muˈrɛna]
piranha	піранья (ж)	[piˈranʲa]
shark	акула (ж)	[aˈkula]
dolphin	дельфін (ч)	[dɛlʲˈfin]
whale	кит (ч)	[kit]
crab	краб (ч)	[krab]
jellyfish	медуза (ж)	[mɛˈduza]
octopus	восьминіг (ч)	[wosʲmiˈniɦ]
starfish	морська зірка (ж)	[morsʲˈka ˈzirka]
sea urchin	морський їжак (ч)	[morsʲˈkij jiˈʒak]
seahorse	морський коник (ч)	[morsʲˈkij ˈkɔnik]
oyster	устриця (ж)	[ˈustriʦʲa]
prawn	креветка (ж)	[krɛˈwɛtka]
lobster	омар (ч)	[oˈmar]
spiny lobster	лангуст (ч)	[lanˈɦust]

92. Amphibians. Reptiles

snake	змія (ж)	[zmiˈʲa]
venomous (snake)	отруйний	[otˈrujnij]
viper	гадюка (ж)	[ɦaˈdʲuka]
cobra	кобра (ж)	[ˈkɔbra]
python	пітон (ч)	[piˈtɔn]
boa	удав (ч)	[uˈdaw]
grass snake	вуж (ч)	[wuʒ]

| rattle snake | гримуча змія (ж) | [ɦriˈmutʃa zmiˈ‖a] |
| anaconda | анаконда (ж) | [anaˈkɔnda] |

lizard	ящірка (ж)	[ˈ‖aɕirka]
iguana	ігуана (ж)	[iɦuˈana]
monitor lizard	варан (ч)	[waˈran]
salamander	саламандра (ж)	[salaˈmandra]
chameleon	хамелеон (ч)	[hamɛlɛˈɔn]
scorpion	скорпіон (ч)	[skorpiˈɔn]

turtle	черепаха (ж)	[tʃɛrɛˈpaha]
frog	жабка (ж)	[ˈʒabka]
toad	жаба (ж)	[ˈʒaba]
crocodile	крокодил (ч)	[krokoˈdɨl]

<h2>93. Insects</h2>

insect	комаха (ж)	[koˈmaha]
butterfly	метелик (ч)	[mɛˈtɛlik]
ant	мураха (ж)	[muˈraha]
fly	муха (ж)	[ˈmuha]
mosquito	комар (ч)	[koˈmar]
beetle	жук (ч)	[ʒuk]

wasp	оса (ж)	[oˈsa]
bee	бджола (ж)	[bdʒoˈla]
bumblebee	джміль (ч)	[dʒmilʲ]
gadfly (botfly)	овід (ч)	[ˈɔwid]

| spider | павук (ч) | [paˈwuk] |
| spider's web | павутиння (с) | [pawuˈtinʲa] |

dragonfly	бабка (ж)	[ˈbabka]
grasshopper	коник (ч)	[ˈkɔnik]
moth (night butterfly)	метелик (ч)	[mɛˈtɛlik]

cockroach	тарган (ч)	[tarˈɦan]
tick	кліщ (ч)	[kliɕ]
flea	блоха (ж)	[ˈbloha]
midge	мошка (ж)	[ˈmɔʃka]

locust	сарана (ж)	[saraˈna]
snail	равлик (ч)	[ˈrawlik]
cricket	цвіркун (ч)	[tswirˈkun]
firefly	світлячок (ч)	[switlʲaˈtʃɔk]
ladybird	сонечко (с)	[ˈsɔnɛtʃko]
cockchafer	хрущ (ч)	[hruɕ]

leech	п'явка (ж)	[ˈpʲawka]
caterpillar	гусениця (ж)	[ˈɦusɛnitsʲa]
earthworm	черв'як (ч)	[tʃɛrwˈʲak]
larva	личинка (ж)	[liˈtʃinka]

FLORA

tree	дерево (с)	['dɛrɛwo]
deciduous (adj)	модринове	[mod'rinowɛ]
coniferous (adj)	хвойне	['hwɔjnɛ]
evergreen (adj)	вічнозелене	[witʃnozɛ'lɛnɛ]

apple tree	яблуня (ж)	['ʲablunʲa]
pear tree	груша (ж)	['hruʃa]
sweet cherry tree	черешня (ж)	[tʃɛ'rɛʃnʲa]
sour cherry tree	вишня (ж)	['wiʃnʲa]
plum tree	слива (ж)	['sliwa]

birch	береза (ж)	[bɛ'rɛza]
oak	дуб (ч)	[dub]
linden tree	липа (ж)	['lipa]
aspen	осика (ж)	[o'sika]
maple	клен (ч)	[klɛn]
spruce	ялина (ж)	[ja'lina]
pine	сосна (ж)	[sos'na]
larch	модрина (ж)	[mod'rina]
fir tree	ялиця (ж)	[ja'litsʲa]
cedar	кедр (ч)	[kɛdr]

poplar	тополя (ж)	[to'pɔlʲa]
rowan	горобина (ж)	[horo'bina]
willow	верба (ж)	[wɛr'ba]
alder	вільха (ж)	['wilʲha]
beech	бук (ч)	[buk]
elm	в'яз (ч)	[wʲaz]
ash (tree)	ясен (ч)	['ʲasɛn]
chestnut	каштан (ч)	[kaʃ'tan]

magnolia	магнолія (ж)	[mah'nɔliʲa]
palm tree	пальма (ж)	['palʲma]
cypress	кипарис (ч)	[kipa'ris]

mangrove	мангрове дерево (с)	['manhrowɛ 'dɛrɛwo]
baobab	баобаб (ч)	[bao'bab]
eucalyptus	евкаліпт (ч)	[ɛwka'lipt]
sequoia	секвоя (ж)	[sɛk'wɔʲa]

| bush | кущ (ч) | [kuɕ] |
| shrub | кущі (мн) | [ku'ɕi] |

| grapevine | виноград (ч) | [wino'ɦrad] |
| vineyard | виноградник (ч) | [wino'ɦradnik] |

raspberry bush	малина (ж)	[ma'lina]
redcurrant bush	порічки (мн)	[po'ritʃki]
gooseberry bush	аґрус (ч)	['agrus]
acacia	акація (ж)	[a'katsiʲa]
barberry	барбарис (ч)	[barba'ris]
jasmine	жасмин (ч)	[ʒas'min]

juniper	ялівець (ч)	[jali'wɛts]
rosebush	трояндовий кущ (ч)	[tro'ʲandowij kuɕ]
dog rose	шипшина (ж)	[ʃip'ʃina]

96. Fruits. Berries

apple	яблуко (с)	['ʲabluko]
pear	груша (ж)	['ɦruʃa]
plum	слива (ж)	['sliwa]
strawberry (garden ~)	полуниця (ж)	[polu'nitsʲa]
sour cherry	вишня (ж)	['wiʃnʲa]
sweet cherry	черешня (ж)	[tʃɛ'rɛʃnʲa]
grape	виноград (ч)	[wino'ɦrad]

raspberry	малина (ж)	[ma'lina]
blackcurrant	чорна смородина (ж)	['tʃorna smo'rɔdina]
redcurrant	порічки (мн)	[po'ritʃki]
gooseberry	аґрус (ч)	['agrus]
cranberry	журавлина (ж)	[ʒuraw'lina]

orange	апельсин (ч)	[apɛlʲ'sin]
tangerine	мандарин (ч)	[manda'rin]
pineapple	ананас (ч)	[ana'nas]
banana	банан (ч)	[ba'nan]
date	фінік (ч)	['finik]

lemon	лимон (ч)	[li'mɔn]
apricot	абрикос (ч)	[abri'kɔs]
peach	персик (ч)	['pɛrsik]
kiwi	ківі (ч)	['kiwi]
grapefruit	грейпфрут (ч)	[ɦrɛjp'frut]

berry	ягода (ж)	['ʲaɦoda]
berries	ягоди (мн)	['ʲaɦodi]
cowberry	брусниця (ж)	[brus'nitsʲa]
wild strawberry	суниця (ж)	[su'nitsʲa]
bilberry	чорниця (ж)	[tʃor'nitsʲa]

97. Flowers. Plants

| flower | квітка (ж) | ['kwitka] |
| bouquet (of flowers) | букет (ч) | [bu'kɛt] |

rose (flower)	троянда (ж)	[tro'ˠanda]
tulip	тюльпан (ч)	[tʲulʲˠpan]
carnation	гвоздика (ж)	[ɦwozˈdɨka]
gladiolus	гладіолус (ч)	[ɦladiˈɔlus]

cornflower	волошка (ж)	[woˈlɔʃka]
harebell	дзвіночок (ч)	[dʒwiˈnɔt͡ʃok]
dandelion	кульбаба (ж)	[kulʲˠbaba]
camomile	ромашка (ж)	[roˈmaʃka]

aloe	алое (ч)	[aˈlɔɛ]
cactus	кактус (ч)	[ˈkaktus]
rubber plant, ficus	фікус (ч)	[ˈfikus]

lily	лілея (ж)	[liˈlɛʲa]
geranium	герань (ж)	[ɦɛˈranʲ]
hyacinth	гіацинт (ч)	[ɦiaˈt͡sɨnt]

mimosa	мімоза (ж)	[miˈmɔza]
narcissus	нарцис (ч)	[narˈt͡sɨs]
nasturtium	настурція (ж)	[nasˈturt͡siʲa]

orchid	орхідея (ж)	[orhiˈdɛʲa]
peony	півонія (ж)	[piˈwɔniʲa]
violet	фіалка (ж)	[fiˈalka]

pansy	братки (мн)	[bratˈkɨ]
forget-me-not	незабудка (ж)	[nɛzaˈbudka]
daisy	стокротки (мн)	[stokˈrɔtkɨ]

poppy	мак (ч)	[mak]
hemp	коноплі (мн)	[koˈnɔpli]
mint	м'ята (ж)	[ˈmʲata]

| lily of the valley | конвалія (ж) | [konˈwaliʲa] |
| snowdrop | пролісок (ч) | [ˈprɔlisok] |

nettle	кропива (ж)	[kropɨˈwa]
sorrel	щавель (ч)	[ɕaˈwɛlʲ]
water lily	латаття (с)	[laˈtattʲa]
fern	папороть (ж)	[ˈpaporotʲ]
lichen	лишайник (ч)	[lɨˈʃajnɨk]

conservatory (greenhouse)	оранжерея (ж)	[oranʒɛˈrɛʲa]
lawn	газон (ч)	[ɦaˈzɔn]
flowerbed	клумба (ж)	[ˈklumba]

plant	рослина (ж)	[rosˈlɨna]
grass	трава (ж)	[traˈwa]
blade of grass	травинка (ж)	[traˈwɨnka]

leaf	листок (ч)	[lɨsˈtɔk]
petal	пелюстка (ж)	[pɛˈlʲustka]
stem	стебло (с)	[stɛbˈlɔ]
tuber	бульба (ж)	[ˈbulʲba]
young plant (shoot)	паросток (ч)	[ˈparostok]

thorn	колючка (ч)	[ko'lʲutʃka]
to blossom (vi)	цвісти	[tswis'ti]
to fade, to wither	в'янути	['wʲʲanuti]
smell (odour)	запах (ч)	['zapah]
to cut (flowers)	зрізати	['zrizati]
to pick (a flower)	зірвати	[zir'wati]

98. Cereals, grains

grain	зерно (с)	[zɛr'nɔ]
cereal crops	зернові рослини (мн)	[zɛrno'wi ros'lini]
ear (of barley, etc.)	колос (ч)	['kɔlos]

wheat	пшениця (ж)	[pʃɛ'nitsʲa]
rye	жито (с)	['ʒito]
oats	овес (ч)	[o'wɛs]
millet	просо (с)	['prɔso]
barley	ячмінь (ч)	[jatʃ'minʲ]

maize	кукурудза (ж)	[kuku'rudza]
rice	рис (ч)	[ris]
buckwheat	гречка (ж)	['ɦrɛtʃka]

pea plant	горох (ч)	[ɦo'rɔh]
kidney bean	квасоля (ж)	[kwa'sɔlʲa]
soya	соя (ж)	['sɔʲa]
lentil	сочевиця (ж)	[sotʃɛ'witsʲa]
beans (pulse crops)	боби (мн)	[bo'bʲi]

COUNTRIES OF THE WORLD

99. Countries. Part 1

Afghanistan	Афганістан (ч)	[afhani'stan]
Albania	Албанія (ж)	[al'baniⁱa]
Argentina	Аргентина (ж)	[arhɛn'tina]
Armenia	Вірменія (ж)	[wir'mɛniⁱa]
Australia	Австралія (ж)	[aw'straliⁱa]
Austria	Австрія (ж)	['awstriⁱa]
Azerbaijan	Азербайджан (ч)	[azɛrbaj'dʒan]
The Bahamas	Багамські острови (мн)	[ba'hamsⁱki ostro'wiⁱ]
Bangladesh	Бангладеш (ч)	[banhla'dɛʃ]
Belarus	Білорусь (ж)	[bilo'rusⁱ]
Belgium	Бельгія (ж)	['bɛlⁱhiⁱa]
Bolivia	Болівія (ж)	[bo'liwiⁱa]
Bosnia and Herzegovina	Боснія і Герцеговина (ж)	['bɔsniⁱa i hɛrtsɛho'wina]
Brazil	Бразилія (ж)	[bra'ziliⁱa]
Bulgaria	Болгарія (ж)	[bol'hariⁱa]
Cambodia	Камбоджа (ж)	[kam'bɔdʒa]
Canada	Канада (ж)	[ka'nada]
Chile	Чилі (ж)	['ʧili]
China	Китай (ч)	[ki'taj]
Colombia	Колумбія (ж)	[ko'lumbiⁱa]
Croatia	Хорватія (ж)	[hor'watiⁱa]
Cuba	Куба (ж)	['kuba]
Cyprus	Кіпр (ж)	[kipr]
Czech Republic	Чехія (ж)	['ʧɛhiⁱa]
Denmark	Данія (ж)	['daniⁱa]
Dominican Republic	Домініканська республіка (ж)	[domini'kansⁱka rɛs'publika]
Ecuador	Еквадор (ч)	[ɛkwa'dɔr]
Egypt	Єгипет (ч)	[ɛ'hipɛt]
England	Англія (ж)	['anhliⁱa]
Estonia	Естонія (ж)	[ɛs'toniⁱa]
Finland	Фінляндія (ж)	[fin'lⁱandiⁱa]
France	Франція (ж)	['frantsiⁱa]
French Polynesia	Французька Полінезія (ж)	[fran'ʦuzⁱka poli'nɛziⁱa]
Georgia	Грузія (ж)	['hruziⁱa]
Germany	Німеччина (ж)	[ni'mɛʧina]
Ghana	Гана (ж)	['hana]
Great Britain	Великобританія (ж)	[wɛlikobri'taniⁱa]
Greece	Греція (ж)	['hrɛtsiⁱa]
Haiti	Гаїті (ч)	[ha'jiti]
Hungary	Угорщина (ж)	[u'hɔrɕina]

100. Countries. Part 2

Iceland	Ісландія (ж)	[is'landi'a]
India	Індія (ж)	['indi'a]
Indonesia	Індонезія (ж)	[indo'nɛzi'a]
Iran	Іран (ч)	[i'ran]
Iraq	Ірак (ч)	[i'rak]
Ireland	Ірландія (ж)	[ir'landi'a]
Israel	Ізраїль (ч)	[iz'raji'l]
Italy	Італія (ж)	[i'tali'a]

Jamaica	Ямайка (ж)	[ja'majka]
Japan	Японія (ж)	[ja'poni'a]
Jordan	Йорданія (ж)	['or'dani'a]
Kazakhstan	Казахстан (ч)	[kazah'stan]
Kenya	Кенія (ж)	['kɛni'a]
Kirghizia	Киргизстан (ч)	[kirɦiz'stan]
Kuwait	Кувейт (ч)	[ku'wɛjt]

Laos	Лаос (ч)	[la'ɔs]
Latvia	Латвія (ж)	['latwi'a]
Lebanon	Ліван (ч)	[li'wan]
Libya	Лівія (ж)	['liwi'a]
Liechtenstein	Ліхтенштейн (ч)	[lihtɛn'ʃtɛjn]
Lithuania	Литва (ж)	[lit'wa]
Luxembourg	Люксембург (ч)	[l'uksɛm'burɦ]

North Macedonia	Македонія (ж)	[makɛ'doni'a]
Madagascar	Мадагаскар (ч)	[madaɦa'skar]
Malaysia	Малайзія (ж)	[ma'lajzi'a]
Malta	Мальта (ж)	['mal'ta]
Mexico	Мексика (ж)	['mɛksika]

Moldova, Moldavia	Молдова (ж)	[mol'dɔwa]
Monaco	Монако (с)	[mo'nako]
Mongolia	Монголія (ж)	[mon'ɦoli'a]
Montenegro	Чорногорія (ж)	[ʧorno'ɦori'a]
Morocco	Марокко (с)	[ma'rɔkko]
Myanmar	М'янма (ж)	['m'anma]

Namibia	Намібія (ж)	[na'mibi'a]
Nepal	Непал (ч)	[nɛ'pal]
Netherlands	Нідерланди (ж)	[nidɛr'landi]
New Zealand	Нова Зеландія (ж)	[no'wa zɛ'landi'a]
North Korea	Північна Корея (ж)	[piw'niʧna ko'rɛ'a]
Norway	Норвегія (ж)	[nor'wɛɦi'a]

101. Countries. Part 3

Pakistan	Пакистан (ч)	[paki'stan]
Palestine	Палестинська автономія (ж)	[palɛ'stins'ka awto'nomi'a]
Panama	Панама (ж)	[pa'nama]

Paraguay	Парагвай (ч)	[paraɦ'waj]
Peru	Перу (ж)	[pɛ'ru]
Poland	Польща (ж)	['pɔlʲɕa]
Portugal	Португалія (ж)	[portu'ɦaliʲa]
Romania	Румунія (ж)	[ru'muniʲa]
Russia	Росія (ж)	[ro'siʲa]

Saudi Arabia	Саудівська Аравія (ж)	[sa'udiwsʲka a'rawiʲa]
Scotland	Шотландія (ж)	[ʃot'landiʲa]
Senegal	Сенегал (ч)	[sɛnɛ'ɦal]
Serbia	Сербія (ж)	['sɛrbiʲa]
Slovakia	Словаччина (ж)	[slo'watʃina]
Slovenia	Словенія (ж)	[slo'wɛniʲa]

South Africa	Південно-Африканська Республіка (ж)	[piw'dɛno afri'kansʲka rɛs'publika]
South Korea	Південна Корея (ж)	[piw'dɛna ko'rɛʲa]
Spain	Іспанія (ж)	[ispaniʲa]
Suriname	Суринам (ч)	[suri'nam]
Sweden	Швеція (ж)	['ʃwɛtsiʲa]
Switzerland	Швейцарія (ж)	[ʃwɛj'tsariʲa]
Syria	Сирія (ж)	['siriʲa]

Taiwan	Тайвань (ч)	[taj'wanʲ]
Tajikistan	Таджикистан (ч)	[tadʒiki'stan]
Tanzania	Танзанія (ж)	[tan'zaniʲa]
Tasmania	Тасманія (ж)	[tas'maniʲa]
Thailand	Таїланд (ч)	[taji'land]
Tunisia	Туніс (ч)	[tu'nis]
Turkey	Туреччина (ж)	[tu'rɛtʃina]
Turkmenistan	Туркменістан (ч)	[turkmɛni'stan]

Ukraine	Україна (ж)	[ukra'jina]
United Arab Emirates	Об'єднані Арабські емірати (мн)	[o'bʔɛdnani a'rabsʲki ɛmi'ratɨ]
United States of America	Сполучені Штати Америки (мн)	[spo'lutʃɛni 'ʃtatɨ a'mɛrikɨ]
Uruguay	Уругвай (ч)	[uruɦ'waj]
Uzbekistan	Узбекистан (ч)	[uzbɛki'stan]

Vatican City	Ватикан (ч)	[wati'kan]
Venezuela	Венесуела (ж)	[wɛnɛsu'ɛla]
Vietnam	В'єтнам (ч)	[wʔɛt'nam]
Zanzibar	Занзібар (ч)	[zanzi'bar]

'MY' Pronoun.

Ae Moï сестрn?
where are my sisters?

Ae Miñ Apyr?
where is my friend?

Він Miñ батько
He is my father.

Моє місто   Моє м'ясо
My City   My meat

Моє село
my Village.

Мог подруга
My female friend.

Miñ будинок Моя сім'я Моє село
My hoose, My family, My village.

Printed in Great Britain
by Amazon

78289010R00059